Anonymous

The Home Guide

Or, a book by 500 ladies, embracing about 1,000 recipes and hints, pertaining to cookery, the household, the sick room, the toilet, etc.

Anonymous

The Home Guide
Or, a book by 500 ladies, embracing about 1,000 recipes and hints, pertaining to cookery, the household, the sick room, the toilet, etc.

ISBN/EAN: 9783744788977

Printed in Europe, USA, Canada, Australia, Japan

Cover: Foto ©Lupo / pixelio.de

More available books at **www.hansebooks.com**

The Home Guide;

OR,

A Book by 500 Ladies,

EMBRACING

ABOUT 1,000 RECIPES AND HINTS,

Pertaining to Cookery, The Household, The Sick Room, The Toilet, Etc.

COMPILED CHIEFLY FROM

"The Home" Department of the Chicago Daily Tribune.

PUBLISHED BY
S. L. TAYLOR, ELGIN, ILL.
1877.

Entered according to an Act of Congress, by
S. L. TAYLOR, ELGIN, ILL.,
In the office of the Congressional Librarian, at
Washington, 1877.

CONTENTS.

Introductory	5–6
Cookery	7–139
Soups	7–11
Fish	12–18
Poultry	18–23
Meats	23–31
Game	31–32
Shell Fish, Oysters, etc.	33–36
Salads	37–38
Vegetables	39–46
Eggs	47–49
Coffee	50–53
Bread	53–66
Cakes, Cookies, etc.	66–89
Frosting, Icing, etc.	90–91
Pies	92–101
Puddings	101–117
Sauces for Puddings, etc.	117–118
Pancakes, Fritters, etc.	119–121
Custard, Blanc Mange, etc.	121–126
Fruits, Jellies, etc.	126–130
Pickles, Sauces, Catsups, etc.	131–134
Confectionery	135–136
Yeasts, Baking Powders, etc.	137–138
Miscellaneous	138–139
Household Hints	140–150
The Toilet	151–157
The Sick Room, etc.	158–160

TO THE LADIES,

WHOSE SKILL AND PRACTICAL GOOD SENSE

Have Contributed so much to the Success and Popularity of "The Home," and who are

THE REAL AUTHORS HEREOF,

This Volume is Respectfully

DEDICATED,

BY THE PUBLISHER.

INTRODUCTORY.

This little volume is sent forth in the confident belief that it is the *Ne Plus Ultra* of Cook Books, or Guides to Housekeepers. Unlike the trashy cook and recipe books vended about the country for $1.50 or $2.00 a copy, "hashed" up from irresponsible sources, more with a view to size and show than to practical utility, the Home Guide is a collection of the *actual and practical experiences*, and *in the language* of 500 lady "Home" keepers. It is a compilation and condensation of the thousands of recipes and hints contributed by the lady readers of the Chicago *Tribune*, and published in the popular "Home" department of that paper during the past two years.

The contents embrace a very wide range of subjects pertaining to Cookery, which is, of course, the chief feature of the book. Every branch of the "culinary art" is treated by practical, successful housekeepers, and in a common sense manner, such as will, upon examination, be appreciated and understood by every lady who looks well to the health and happiness of her family.

The "art" of good cooking is a most valuable acquirement to every household. It not only contrib-

INTRODUCTORY.

utes to health, good temper and domestic peace, but it saves many dollars in grocers' bills. Great quantities of good food is wasted in American kitchens, for the sole reason that housekeepers lack the valuable accomplishment of knowing how to prepare it in various and inviting forms.

In the other Departments of the book will be found many valuable Recipes and Hints upon various subjects pertaining to the Household, the Toilet, and the Sick Room. And, finally, although unpretentious in size, the reader will find upon due examination that "The Home Guide" is rich and voluminous in practical and useful information.

COOKERY.

SOUP.

AS an introductory to the soup department, the following letter from "the best unprofessional cook in Chicago," is given:

Mrs. Sarah L., of Chicago.

I believe it was nearly a year ago that I wrote my first letter to the *Tribune*, the burden of which was *soup*. If I have a hobby, this is it. A Frenchman once said, "Vat a peoples are ze Americans. Zesty kind of religions and but one kinds of soup. Mon dieu!" And, I have often thought, if we had one kind of religion, perhaps, and 30 kinds of soup, we should be a healthier people.

Now, knowing that the circles of readers has increased marvelously since I first talked about soups, I must beg of you, Mr. Editor, to let me return to my old subject, for it lays very near my heart, and urge upon mothers of young children to adopt this method of preparing soup for their principal meal in the middle of the day.

If dinner is to be served at 12 o'clock, the piece of meat, costing 20 cents, must be put on the fire at 8, in about three quarts of cold water. After it has boiled up, skim off everything that may rise, as well as the grease, if it should be a fatish piece of meat. Then peel and cut an onion in pieces, and salt, about a great spoonful. Let it boil slowly all the time. In an hour or so peel and cut in slices 2 potatoes, $\frac{1}{4}$ a small turnip, and a piece of carrot. They must all boil up fine; about 2 quarts of water must always be kept over the meat. At the same time the meat is put on the range, another kettle, holding about 2 or 3 quarts, containing $2\frac{1}{2}$ cups of split peas, with just enough water to keep them from burning, must be set in a place where they will just boil. When more water is needed add the soup or bouillons—always boiling. About 20 minutes before dinner is to be served, pour all the liquor from the meat into the peas, which will make a soup about as thick as flour porridge. If not salt enough add more, and a little pepper. When the family is seated around the table, let the girl dish the soup hot from the kettle into each soup-plate. This soup must be hot or it is not good.

Bean and tomato soup I make in the same way, only the tomatoes will cook in an hour all that they need. These 3 kinds are good and nourishing in the spring, and every child coming home from school should have a plate to set his or her hungry stomach to work upon. The rest of the dinner the stomach is then prepared for.

In my family I have some kind of soup almost every day in the week, and I believe it has made me a new stomach in the last 6 years. I was brought up on mince pies, roast beef, cocoanut cake and preserves. Now I eat my soup, a piece of the soup meat, with mustard, horse radish, or a little catsup, some good mashed potatoes, a puree, or some well-cooked vegetable, a pudding for dessert, and I have no more dyspepsia, and my children are the pictures of health. I don't mean that the above is always our dinner, but sometimes. Ladies, try it. We have all been brought up on too rich food. The nearer we live to nature the better bodies and minds we shall have.

I was reading a book the other day, and came across this old English proverb: "Eggs of an hour, fish of ten, bread of a day, wine of a year, a woman of 15, and a friend of 30." I might agree with the proverb in some respects, but a woman and friend are good for nothing until 40. So says "my man."

Turkey Soup.
Bertha Carlyle, Hyde Park.

Save all the bones and break the backbone into 2 or 3 pieces; boil these in a little more water than you want soup, for an hour; then skim out the bone, and put in the meat, cut in very small pieces, and boil a few moments more; then season with a little salt and pepper.

COOKERY—SOUP. 9

Mock Turtle.
"Cook," Rockford, Ills.

Take ¼ a calf's head, fresh and unstripped of skin; remove the brains, and clean the head carefully in hot water, leaving it in cold water for an hour; then put into 6 quarts of warm water, with 2 pounds of veal, ditto pork, a roasted onion stuck with cloves, a rind of lemon, 2 sliced carrots, a bunch of herbs and a head of celery; let it boil slowly 2 hours; then take out the head and pork; make forcemeat balls of the brains and tongue; break the bones of the head; put all into the soup, and boil two hours more. Put into a small stewpan a piece of butter, onions sliced thin, with parsley, mace and allspice; add flour to thicken, and stir in soup slowly. Boil gently 1 hour more; pass through a sieve; season with salt, cayenne, lemon juice and a pint of Maderia wine. Add mushrooms, if desired, and serve with lemons cut in quarters.

Cheat Oyster.
M. A. D., Chicago.

Take of tomatoes 1 pint, canned or fresh; take a large teacup of nice white codfish, picked up fine; add to this 3 pints water; a small tablespoonful good sweet butter; when these have boiled 20 minutes, add 1 pint fresh milk—having ready ½ teaspoonful baking soda. Use immediately. The taste is similar to oysters or lobsters; all taste of tomatoes and fish are gone.

Tomato Soup.
Mrs. M. J. T., Chicago.

To 1 pint canned tomatoes, or 4 large raw ones, cut up fine, add 1 quart of boiling water, and let them boil. Then add one teaspoon of soda, when it will foam; immediately add 1 pint of sweet milk, with salt, pepper, and plenty of butter. When this boils, add 8 small crackers, and serve. It tastes very much like oyster soup.

Turkey Soup.
E. A. E., Chicago.

Put all the bones, the scraps of meat, and the dressing of the turkey in a kettle, with enough water to cover them. Let it boil for 2 hours. When nearly done add the tops of some celery chopped fine, and a teaspoonful of currie powder. When it is done, strain and set on the table hot. It makes a very rich, nice dish.

White Soup.
Amie M. Hale, M. D., Chicago.

Boil a veal bone 3 hours with turnip, celery, onion, carrots, and whatever suitable thing else you have which will not turn it dark. Strain and boil again; just before you serve it add a pint of cream or milk, with 3 eggs well beaten; remove from the stove and stir rapidly.

Vegetable Soup.
Mrs. Sarah L., Chicago.

Scrape 2 carrots, an onion, ¼ of a cabbage, and 2 turnips. Cut them in pieces a little larger than dice. Put the pieces in a large sauce-pan with a little butter and water; let it cook ½ hour; then cut your potatoes in the same way. Take your meat out of the soup-kettle, skim off the grease and put all into your broth, and let cook another ½ hour. In the language of the average school-girl, "it's perfectly lovely."

Beef Soup.
Myrtle, Dundee, Ills.

Cut the meat off the bone, and place it, with some suet, in the kettle to fry until brown. Then put the bone in and cover with cold water. Add ½ cup of barley, 1 onion and a turnip, put in the barley at *once*, and cook slowly until about ½ an hour before dinner, then cut the vegetables very fine, and cook them the ½ hour.

"Soup Medley."
"Mrs. Emily," Eau Claire, Wis.

No. 1—1 pint of good gravy, 3 cups boiling water, a slice of turnip and ¼ an onion cut in small bits, 2 grated crackers. Simmer half an hour.

No. 2—Cut off the narrow ends from 2 or 3 sirloin steaks, chop them into morsels and put in a stewpan with a little salt, a tablespoonful of rice and a pint of cold water. Let it come slowly to a simmer, and simmer slowly for 3 hours. Then add water enough to make quart of soup, a tablespoonful of tomato catsup, and a little browned flour mixed with the yolk of an egg.

No. 3—Pare and slice very thin 4 good-sized potatoes, pour over them 2 cups of boiling water, and simmer gently until the potatoes are dissolved. Add salt, a lump of nice butter and a pint of sweet milk with a dust of pepper. Boil up once, and serve.

No. 4—1 pint meat broth, 1 pint boiling water, slice in an onion, or a parsnip, or half a turnip—or all 3 if liked—boil until the vegetables are soft, add a little salt if needed, and a tablespoonful of Halford sauce.

No. 5—Let green corn—in the time of green corn—be grated, and to a pint of it put a pint of rich milk, a pint of water, a little butter, salt and pepper. Boil gently for 15 or 20 minutes.

Noodle Soup.
"Mrs. C. G. M.," Chicago.

Break 2 eggs into a bowl; beat until light, adding a pinch of salt; then work in flour (with your hand) until you have a very stiff dough; turn it on your molding board, and work until it is as smooth as glass; pinch off a piece the size of a walnut, and roll it as thin as paper; then with a sharp knife cut off very narrow strips; proceed in the same way until all your dough is cut. Have prepared some good veal, chicken, or any other kind of broth, well seasoned, $\frac{1}{2}$ an hour before you serve dinner; drop in the noodles. Be sure the soup is boiling. Add a little parsley. If the noodles are made according to directions, they will be found far superior to maccaroni.

Tomato Soup.
"Mrs. E. S. P.," Burlington, Iowa.

Put a tablespoonful of drippings or butter in a stewpan; cut an onion fine and fry in the butter; then add one pint of tomatoes, pepper, salt and a teaspoonful of allspice; cut a round steak in two and lay on the tomatoes; cover closely and let it simmer for three hours.

FISH.

Boiled Fish.
Delmonico's Method.

FROM a reliable source, the following is presented as Delmonico's method for boiling fish:

Fish should be washed as little as possible, and whitefish, after being cleaned and wiped with a damp cloth, should have the stomach stuffed with salt for an hour or two before cooking. Fish should be put on in cold water, so that the inner part may be sufficiently done, and it is also less liable to break. This rule holds good, except for very small fish, or for salmon boiled in slices, when boiling water should be used. The time may be easily known when it is ready by drawing up the fish-plate and trying if it will separate from the bone. A little salt and vinegar should always be put into the water. Some prefer their fish boiled in what is called a court bouillon, and this is how it is done: Lay the fish in the kettle with enough cold water to cover it, add a glass of wine or vinegar, some sliced carrot and onions, pepper, salt and a laurel leaf, a bunch of parsley, a fagot of sweet herbs, or some of the same tied up in a muslin bag. These seasonings impart a fine flavor to most boiled fish, excepting salmon, and for fresh-water fish it is considered very useful for getting rid of the muddy taste they often have.

Boiled Fish.
Mrs. M. A. D., Chicago.

After well cleansing a good-sized fish, put into a fish-kettle, and set into a pot of boiling water well salted; let it boil for 20 minutes; take of vinegar sufficient to cover; put into the vinegar 1 ounce of cloves, 1 of allspice and 1 of pepper whole; boil all together for 15 minutes; when nearly cold pour over the fish; let it stand for 2 or 3 hours before using.

Baked Fish.

Mrs. W. S. G., Baraboo, Wis.

Scale, wash and wipe dry, inside and out, a 2 or 3 pound fish. Make a stuffing as follows: One pint grated bread; 2 tablespoonfuls melted butter; pepper and salt to taste; 1 raw egg; a little celery salt; 1 onion, chopped fine, is, to my taste, an improvement, but can be omitted if not liked. Care should be taken not to wet the bread-crumbs; the egg and melted butter will moisten sufficiently. Tie over the fish thin slices of salt pork; fill a dripping pan ½ full hot water; then, if you have not a wire grate, place the gridiron on the pan, and after laying the fish on the gridiron cover all with another pan; bake in a hot oven till the pork is well shrivelled; then remove the upper tin, allowing your fish to brown. 1½ hours will cook thoroughly, if a steady fire is kept.

Mrs. E. G., Geneva.

First, dip the fish quickly in boiling water; then wipe the scales off; rinse in cold water; wipe it dry; sprinkle salt both inside and out, about as much as you would for steaks. Then dip it in flour; place the pan that you are going to bake it in in the stove with a piece of butter in it the size of an egg. Let it melt so that it covers the pan. Your pan should be about the length of your fish; if larger, the butter will be apt to burn. Place your fish in it, the inside of it next to the pan. Put it in a hot oven, and bake 1 hour, if it is a large fish, less time if smaller. It should be well done and of a nice brown color.

Mrs. S. D. L., Chicago.

Skin and bone the fish, by running a sharp knife along the back. Spread over dripping-pan a thin layer of butter, ½ an onion in fine pieces. Lay the fish upon it, and pour over the fish 1 tablespoonful of vinegar or Catawba wine. For the sauce, rub butter, the size of a walnut, and flour together, add a cup of the broth or hot water, the juice of the fish, 2 or 3 mushrooms, if you have them. Turn this mixture over the fish, dust with bread crumbs, salt and pepper, and bake a few minutes or until a little brown. Garnish with pieces of bread cut heart-shape.

COOKERY—FISH.

Mrs. Sarah L., Chicago.

Dry with a towel, and put belly to back in dripping-pan, into which you have previously cut up 2 slices of salt pork in inch pieces. Make a stuffing as for veal. Stuff, putting only a little in. Now pour over the fish a spoonful of lemon-juice or good vinegar. After a little, baste with a little soup-broth. Don't let the fish dry all up, and don't put a drop of water on it. Make your sauce as for veal cutlets, omitting the lemon juice, but add ¼ cup of milk and cut up 2 hard-boiled eggs into it. When done, also add the fish-juice. A little parsley chopped fine in the sauce, we like. Garnish with hard-boiled eggs and sprigs of parsley, mounted by little carpels of lemon.

M. A. D., Chicago.

Take bread crumbs sufficient for the size of the fish; beat 2 or 3 eggs; pepper and salt; add 1 bunch of parsley, fresh, and chopped fine; mix all together well; add a small piece of butter; put all into the fish and sew up. If any of the dressing is left, put into the bake-pan; add a pint of boiling water; put into a hot oven; baste every 10 or 15 minutes for an hour, when it will be well cooked and nicely flavored.

E. L. M., Chicago.

Buy a 2-pound white fish. If the gills are red, eyes full, body firm and stiff, the fish is good. Scale it, cut off the head, and split the fish nearly down to the tail. make a dressing of bread-crumbs, a little butter, pepper and salt, slightly moistened with water. Stuff the fish with this; then bind it together with fine cotton cord or tape, 3 inches apart. Lay the fish on a wire gridiron in a dripping-pan, and pour around it a little water and melted butter. With a spoon dip this up and pour over the fish frequently. Bake 1 hour. Serve with the gravy of the fish or drawn butter.

Fried Fish.
M. A. D., Chicago.

When the fish is properly cleansed, instead of putting it into a small quantity of fat or grease, wipe dry; then rub with plenty of salt and pepper; let it lay an hour or two before using; roll in corn-meal or flour; have ready i2t sufficient for it to swim in; the fat must be boiling-hot; put the fish in whole, or cut in pieces. It will come out nicely browned, and not filled with fat, as in the ordinary way of frying.

Frying Fish.
N. M. G , New York.

The artistic mode of frying fish is what is called the wet process, which is simply boiling it in fat. Butter should never be used, as the color never is good. Lard is considered by many to be the best frying medium, but Careme, the great French cook, gives the preference to beef fat—not, however, the dripping from the roast, but lard made by melting beef suet. We recommend as best and most economical drippings from the joints while roasting, poured into boiling water, and removed in a cake when cold. The great point is to have the fat at a proper temperature before the article to be fried is put in. The skillful cook can see the blue smoke rising just at the boiling point, and then she knows it is time to put in her fish; but for those who are only acquiring experience it is safer to throw in a bit of bread, and if it takes a fine color in a minute or so, then the fat is hot enough, and the fish may be put in. This is the cardinal point of successful frying, as otherwise the fish will be flabby and greasy instead of crisp and appetizing. Another point to be attended to is that the fat be deep enough in the pan to cover the fish, which should be put in a wire basket that will fit easily into the pan of fat, and then no turning is required. When done strain it into boiling water; when cold take it off in a cake, and put it by to fry fish again.

Sauces for Fish.
Georgia H., Chicago.

To serve with fish: 1 cup vinegar; 1 cup water; yolks 2 eggs; 1 large spoon butter; 1 spoonful mustard and corn-starch blended; sugar, salt and pepper; mix all cold; heat it gradually and boil for a minute. This dressing is also nice, when cold, with salmon, lobster, lettuce, etc.

Fish Sauce.
Mrs. M. G. L., Chicago.

Take a pint of milk and the fish drippings mixed; a

little salt and pepper; mix until smooth, 2 ounces of butter and two teaspoonfuls of flour; stir into the liquor when boiling; have ready a hard-boiled egg, chopped fine, to add when ready for the table.

Stewed Codfish.
Mrs. C. E., Minonk, Ills.

First, be sure and pick the meat off from the bones; then let it stand in water for 15 minutes; then take it out of the water and put in milk. To make the quantity you may need, beat 3 eggs and put into it a pint of milk, a piece of butter half the size of an egg; thicken this with a tablespoonful of flour stirred up with a very little water. As soon as it boils it is done.

Codfish Balls.
E. B., Coldwater, Mich.

Cut up the fish into small bits, enough to make 2 even pints; remove every bone; pour cold water over it to rinse it off, and soak in cold water about 1½ hours; then drain the water off; put it cooking with sufficient boiling water to cover it; let it simmer, not boil, for 20 minutes; then drain the water all off; pour in 1½ pints of new milk; add a lump of butter size of hen's egg. Take ¼ pint of milk; rub into it three tablespoons of flour—every lump must be dissolved; stir in two eggs, well beaten, and a little black pepper. When the milk boils up, stir in this mixture; cook 5 minutes longer, stirring the most of the time. Serve immediately in a warmed vegetable-dish. This quantity will be sufficient for a family of six, and enough left for codfish balls.

Busy Bee, Ottumwa, Iowa.

Pick up fine a teacupful nice white codfish, freshen over night in water, pour away this in the morning, add ¼ teacup of fresh water, 1 large spoonful of butter, 2 eggs, beat all well together and heat till hot, but do not boil; mash and season nicely some potatoes, stir into the codfish mixture till stiff enough to put in flat cakes, and fry in hot butter a nice brown, should be turned once.

E. D., Chicago.

After dinner, take the mashed potatoes (of which

there should be a double quantity prepared for dinner), and fish that is left, using ⅓ fish and ⅔ potatoes. Stir and beat them together while warm, till evenly mixed. When cold—for the mixture will be so soft it cannot be handled while warm—make them into cakes ¾ inch thick and as large around as a teacup; put them in a cool place for breakfast. In the morning, roll them in flour; have plenty of butter in the frying-pan just hot enough not to burn; fry quickly to a nice brown on both sides. Turn carefully that they may keep their shape. Serve as soon as done.

Mrs. S. W. L., Tuscola, Ills.

Take of nice white codfish about 2 pounds; put into a kettle with sufficient cold water to cover the fish, and let it boil till perfectly tender; then remove to a pan of cold water; the fish can then be easily separated from bones, skin, etc. Place in an earthen or bright tin mixing-pan, and mash fine, with about double the quantity of nicely steamed potatoes, and 3 or 4 slices of light bread crummed, or previously soaked in milk; add 2 eggs and a tea cup of butter, with black pepper to suit taste. Mash and mix thoroughly, and make as moist as is wished with sweet milk. It is sometimes necessary to add a little salt. Make into flat balls, and fry in hot lard, as you would mush. This mixture will keep in cool weather a number of days.

Anna Bell, Springfield.

Take ½ a codfish, put in a pot, fill with cold water at night, in the morning pour off the water, fill up with fresh water, stand it on the back of the stove for 3 hours let it come to a scalding heat, not boiling. Take off the skin and pick out the bones, put in a tray and chop fine, have potatoes boiled and chop with the fish, double the quantity of potatoes to the fish, mix well together, make in balls, with the hands flattening them a little, have your frying pan hot, with a tablespoonful of lard; fry to a nice brown.

Bechamel Sauce.
Mrs. Sarah L., Chicago.

This sauce is good for almost everything, such as carrots, turnips, asparagus, fish, and, with sugar and wine or brandy added, is good for steamed puddings, cake pudding, rice, etc., etc. Mix cold, and well together, in a tin saucepan, 2 ounces of butter, a tablespoonful of flour; then add a pint of milk; stir continually, and, when thickened, take off the fire. Beat the yolk of an egg in a cup, with a teaspoonful of water. Turn into the sauce and mix well; salt a little and pepper for vegetables; but for puddings, nutmeg and brandy or wine.

POULTRY.

Selecting Fowls.
S. H. M., Chicago.

In selecting a goose or duck, take hold of the toes and pull them apart; if the web separates easily it is young, but if it requires any very great amount of physical force to separate, lay it one side—'tis an old fowl, and you will reap no profit from its purchase, unless you are keeping boarders. Turkeys may be selected by pressing the end of the breast bone. If they are young there is a gristle at the end which will readily yield to the pressure—if old, the end will be found hard and sharp, and you cannot bend it. By strictly following these instructions no one need ever buy an old fowl.

Broiled Chicken.
F., Chicago.

Split down the back; pound lightly; put on the gridiron; lay a tin baking-pan over the chicken; set on the pan a flatiron—the weight will hold the bird in place and keep in the juices. Chicken cooked in this way will be tender and eat well warm or cold. Serve with with hot apple-sauce.

Fried Chicken.
Aunt Lucy, Chicago.

Cut your chicken to pieces according to the size; if very young, just in half; if good size, divide at the joints; see that it is thoroughly cleaned. Wipe it with a clean bit of muslin. Beat up 2 eggs, have a plate of flour, dip each piece first in the flour, then in the egg, season with salt and pepper, here pour lard hissing hot in your skillet, put your chicken in; when brown on one side turn it, brown the other, place upon the platter, mix a tablespoon of flour smoothly into a cup of sweet milk, pour into the fat, stir, boil a few minutes, pour it over the chicken, and I guess anybody's husband will think it pretty good. I fry veal cutlets the same way.

Boned Turkey.
Mrs. M., Chicago.

First, make the stuffing to suit the family taste. I took tenderloin—not too lean—chopped it fine; a teacup of cracker crumbs; 2 eggs; a pint of oysters; some summer savory; pepper and salt; mix all well; had my large needle and stout thread handy, with some two-inch-wide soft bleached old cotton cloth. Now for your turkey. It being well cleaned and singed, be careful not to break the outside skin. Cut off the legs so as to cut all the tendons where they join the drumstick. Cut the first joint from the wing; leave a good length of skin for the neck. Every bone must be taken out from the inside. Beginning with the legs, cut each ligament at the side bone joint, strip the knife close along the bone, so as to cut the flesh clean off, and draw the bone out; when both legs are boneless, follow along the back, breast and wings. The neck is more difficult, but get it out nicely as you can. Now your turkey is one shapeless *slump;* but begin stuffing at the neck, from the inside; having tied securely the skin to prevent escape, fill out the wings, breast, body and legs. Now sew up the skin; bandage it in a shapely manner with your strips, not *too tight,* for fear of the stuffing swelling so as to burst the skin; salt and pepper the outside and steam until perfectly tender. If it's an old chap steam 4 or 5 hours. When done, put a tin plate and a couple of flat-irons on top of it to press until cold. Then cut in nice thin slices.

Mrs. S., Fon du Lac, Wis.

Buy a turkey, one that has not been drawn, so as to

have no openings in it if possible; if drawn, sewing up openings firmly before boning; 2 chickens, 1 beef tongue, 1 can oysters, 1 pound fresh, lean side pork. Have the turkey frozen and thawed, the tongue boiled and skinned, the pork roasted, the oysters taken out of the liquor, the chickens cut in small pieces, and put on to boil with just water enough to cover. Lay the turkey on its breast; cut off the legs and wings at first joint; cut down the whole length of the back, and with a sharp knife scrape the meat at each side from the bones; throw the bones in with the chickens to boil. now for the filling: First, lay the whole tongue to form the breast; clear all the chicken meat from the bones; cut the pork in small pieces; fill up your turkey, legs, wings and all (first tying ends of legs and wings tight), with chicken, pork and oysters, and a little dressing, have the chicken liquor well boiled and seasoned, and strain it into the turkey, which will form a jelly. Sew up the turkey firmly; turn it over and shape it nicely with the hands. Tie a cord tightly to the neck, and draw it round and tie it to the right wing close to the body. Tie down legs and wings, inserting skewers if you have them. Sew around it a piece of strong cloth, and steam or roast, and leave the cloth on till cold. Carve cold in round, thin slices, commencing at the neck.

Boiled Goose.
Mrs. D. H. H., Chicago.

Dress and singe, put into a deep dish, cover with boiling milk and leave over night. In the morning wash off the milk, and put the goose into cold water on the fire; when boiling hot take it off, wash it in warm water and dry with a cloth. This process takes out the oil. Fill the body with a dressing of bread crumbs seasoned with pepper, salt, butter and two chopped onions, if relished, and a little sage. Put the goose into cold water and boil gently until tender. Serve with giblet sauce, and with pickles, or acid jellies.

Cousin German, Chicago.

Cook four calf's feet in 3 quarts of water slowly until done; strain it. Now put goose in a pot, pour over it the broth of the calf's feet and so much water that the goose is well covered by it; add some vinegar, spices, salt and onion, and the half peel of a lemon; cover it and boil slow until the goose is soft. Let it cool off in the broth, take out the goose after it is cold, cut all the meat off the bones and lay it nicely in a deep earthen dish. Take all the fat of the broth, taste it, add more vinegar and salt if necessary; let it run through a cloth, and pour it over the meat. It will be nice and stiff after 24 hours, and you eat it cold with bread or cracker. If you can get gelatine it will be so much simpler to prepare it. Boil the goose in water, vinegar and spices as above; after the goose is soft add 3 ounces of gelatine dissolved in cold water, and proceed just as before. The toughest meat will get tender, if boiled with vinegar. American cooks always steam the goose before roasting. Try it once without steaming. Rub it with salt in and outside; put a little water in your frying pan, and roast it in a hot oven 2 or 3 hours, according to the size, and if it is a young goose you will find it superb.

Pressed Chicken.

Gypsy, Ionia, Mich.

Boil 1 chicken until tender; chop fine; season well with pepper, salt and butter, put into a cloth; put a weight upon it and press like head cheese.

Beatrice, Iowa.

Boil fowls until tender. Remove the meat from the bones and chop very fine, keeping the dark and white meat separate. Boil the liquor down until it will jelly; place in a deep buttered dish a layer of the dark meat; season with salt and pepper and cover with liquor; then a layer of white meat seasoned, and cover with the liquor. Use the liquor when full, put a weight on it, and it will mold firmly.

Maud H., Milwaukee.

Boil a chicken thoroughly; skin it and pick it to pieces; season with salt and pepper; put in a bag, and place it under a press; let it remain over night, and next day it will be ready for use.

Chicken Pie.
Isadora, Monroe, Mich.

Make the crust like baking-powder biscuit, only a trifle shorter. Roll half an inch thick and line a 4 quart tin-pan with it. Have ready 2 small chickens, boiled till tender. Place the pieces of chicken smoothly in the pan; sprinkle salt, and pepper, and a little flour over them; add a few pieces of butter, size of a hazelnut, about a large tablespoonful in all; pour on a little of the liquor they were boiled in; then roll the top crust rather more than half-inch thick; cut large stars or air-holes in it. Bake till crust is thoroughly done.

Fried Chicken with Oysters.

Take a nice tender chicken, open it down the back, and after cleaning it well pound all the bones flat; wash, and wipe it dry on a clean towel; then season with pepper and salt, and fry slowly in sweet lard until tender, and a fine brown on both sides. Then put it on a dish where it will keep warm. Pour off the lard in the pan and any brown particles that may remain; then add ¼ pint of hot water and flour enough to make the gravy of the proper consistency. Have ready about 25 large oysters, which remove from their liquor and put into the pan with the gravy; let them simmer until their gills begin to shrivel, observing to stir them all of the time. When done, pour them over the chicken and send to the table hot.

Chicken Pie.

Cut up the chickens by unjointing them; soak thoroughly in weak salt water; wash thoroughly; put 3 chickens into a kettle with 2 quarts of water and 3 teaspoonfuls of salt. Boil ½ an hour. Make a crust by rubbing ½ a pound of lard into 2 quarts of flour. Take two teacupfuls of sour cream and a teaspoonful and a half of soda; knead quite hard, and roll out half an inch thick. A 4-quart pudding dish will answer to bake in; bring the edge of the crust a little above the rim of the dish; arrange the chicken by packing closely around the dish; if you are fond of pepper, sprinkle some over each layer of chicken; ½ a pound of butter, cut up in lumps and scattered among the meat, is a **great** improvement when the chicken is all in the dish;

stir some flour into the gravy and turn over the chicken; then roll out the upper crust and put over the whole, pinching it closely with the under crust that comes over the rim; prick the top crust for the steam to escape. Bake slowly for 1¼ hours and serve hot. It is delicious.

MEATS.

Beefsteak Fried.
Theo. C. C., Chicago.

TAKE either porterhouse, tenderloin or sirloin steak, not more than 1 inch thick; remove the bone; cut it into pieces about the size of the palm of your hand; have your pan *perfectly clean;* put it over the fire with a very little lard, or what is better, the fat of the steak—on no account use butter. Have pan quite hot, but not smoking; if the pan smoke the grease is burning, which will spoil the flavor your steak; remove the pan and wait a little; have it just hot enough to "siss," but not to smoke; now put in your steak, and turn just as soon as it shows brown—once only! never turn a steak more than once, and do most of the cooking on the second side, leaving it in a very few minutes for those who like it rare, longer for those who like it better done; but don't allow it to stay in the pan one second after it is done enough; remove it to the platter, spread a little nice butter on it, and pepper and salt it. Pour the gravy in the pan into the dish, but not over the meat. The rules to be observed in cooking are these: buy the best steak; *never* pound it; pounding bruises the fibres and lets the juice of the meat escape, and steak without juice is like a woman without a head—no account. Have the pan just hot enough to cicatrize the outside, which will prevent the juice from escaping; don't allow it to lay in hot butter it done this renders it tough and fine, so not cook it till the thing—standing spoils it. To be good must be eaten as soon as cooked; if it *must* stand a little while, **put it in a warm place.**

A. E. D., Chicago.

Have your skillet very hot, and fry your steak with very little butter, just long enough to brown each side. Fill up with boiling water, cover, and let it stew two hours. Take up the steak, thicken the gravy, season to taste, and pour over the meat.

Mock Duck.
Mrs. M. J. T., Chicago.

Take the round of beefsteak, salt and pepper either side, prepare bread or crackers with oysters or without, as for stuffing a turkey; lay your stuffing on the meat; sew up and roast about an hour; and if you do not see the wings and legs you will think you have roast duck.

To Cook Dried Beef.
Mrs. J. M. P., LaSalle, Ills.

Cut in thin slices, place it in the spider and pour hot water on it, thicken with a little flour and water stirred smoothly in. Then season with butter, salt and pepper, boil about 5 minutes, and while boiling break in 1 or 2 eggs and stir all together. Halve and butter some warm biscuit, place in a deep dish and pour the mixture upon them.

Cold Meats.
Mrs. Emily G., Eau Claire, Wis.

Remains of boiled ham, mutton, roast beef, etc., are good chopped finely with hard boiled eggs, 2 heads lettuce, a bit of onion, and seasoned with mustard, oil, vinegar, and, if needed, more salt. Fix it smoothly in a salad dish, and adorn the edges with sprigs of parseley or leaves of curled lettuce. Keep by the ice or in a cool place until wanted.

Sweet Breads.
Barry Grey, Chicago.

Wash clean and let drip; broil on a gridiron, or fry in a little butter and pepper salt and butter just before they are brought in. If you place them a moment in the oven, the seasoning seems to go through them better.

Beef Spiced.
"Old Housekeeper," Chicago.

Spiced round: For a small round—say 25 pounds—

mix in a jar or bowl that can be covered 2 pounds common salt; 1 pound dark brown sugar; ¼ pound ground allspice: 1 ounce ground cloves; two ounces black pepper; one teaspoonful cayenne. A wooden bowl or unpainted tub, that will just hold the round, will be required. Fill the hole from which the marrow bone was taken with marrow or nice fat. Bind into nice shape with strips of cotton and skewers. First rub with a tablespoonful of powdered saltpetre on both sides and in all crevices; leave for 24 hours (it should be in a cool, dry place, that will not freeze). Then rub daily with some of the above mixture for 2 or 3 weeks, turning every 2 days and ladling its own liquor over it. When ready to cook the round, provide a tin dish that will just hold it. Place small pieces of hard wood to keep the meat from sticking to the tin underneath; also chopped vegetables, carrots, onions, celery-tops, and suet or drippings. Some of these should also be thickly strewed on the top. Cover all with a coarse paste rolled to keep moist and retain their flavor, and bake 6 hours in a moderate oven. When done, take off the paste cover; remove the vegetables, etc., and put on the round heavy weights until quite cold. Slice thinly.

Pot Pie.
Mrs. C. B. K., Chicago.

Boil 2 or 3 pounds of nice fat beef. When nearly done add some potatoes, turnips and a head of cabbage, cut in 8 or 10 pieces. Season with pepper and salt while cooking. Serve very hot with apple sauce.

Jelly Cheese.
Aunt Fanny, Denver.

Two sets of pigs' feet put into hot, salted water, sufficient to cover them; boil slowly until the meat falls from the bone. Then put the feet on a dish and take out all the bones; cut the meat into small pieces and return to the kettle in which they were boiled, with the liquor; then season with salt, pepper, sage, savory and sweet marjoram; stir all well together, and let it simmer slowly 20 minutes; then put into deep dishes. When cold, cut into slices, eat cold or hot, with vinegar.

Head Cheese.
Aunt Fanny, Denver.

Clean the legs nicely and boil by themselves, so that when done there will be plenty of the liquor. Boil the upper head, minus ears, eyes and nose, with considerable lean meat, tenderloin is best, and when done remove bones and skin from head and legs; chop the lean; salt and pepper to suit the taste; add the liquor the legs were boiled in, and last, but not least, a teacupful of vinegar and a teacupful of catsup to every gallon. When thoroughly cold it can be cut out in slices.

Pudding Chop.
Mrs. F. B. P., Chicago.

One pound salt pork, skin off the rind, chop fine with 2 pounds of bread crumbs, moisten with water until thin enough to stir like cake dough; add 3 eggs well beaten, pepper, 1 teaspoonful of soda dissolved in water; add a little flour; turn this mixture into a pudding-dish and bake one hour, with slow fire. Serve hot or cold.

To Make Sausage.
Mrs. J. T. S., Bloomington, Ills.

For every 12 pounds of meat use 6 ounces of salt, 1 ounce of black pepper, a tablespoonful of powdered saltpeter, half a teaspoonful of red pepper, and 4 ounces of sage. The sage and red pepper are not essential, and may be omitted by those who do not fancy them. These proportions should be tried on a small scale first, before seasoning the whole batch, to see whether it suits.

To Cook Tongue.
Georgia H., Chicago.

French receipt for cooking tongue: After boiling it as usual, until tender, cut into small pieces and brown with flour and butter. Then add some of the stock; season highly; let it boil a few moments and serve hot.

Croquettes.
"Sojourner," Minneapolis.

Cold bits of meat can be finely chopped, and with

bread crumbs, salt and pepper added, mixed with gravy or milk, and made into balls or croquettes, and delicately browned in a skillet for tea. This same prepared meat need not be recooked, but put into a bowl, pressed with a heavy weight for a few hours, and then sliced down like "head-cheese" for tea, called "pressed meat."

Veal Loaf.
Mrs. H. R., Galesburg, Ills.

Two pounds veal, chopped fine; 2 coffee-cups bread crumbs; 2 eggs; 1 even tablespoon of salt and pepper mixed; sage to taste; a little butter; bake about 1 hour; slice quite thin. The secret of having it slice off thin, without breaking, is pressing it down very firmly in the dish before baking.

Baked Veal-Ham.
S. C., Dubuque, Iowa.

Bone a breast of veal. Chop the meat very fine. Chop an equal quantity of cold boiled ham, and boil 6 eggs and chop fine. Butter a deep pan. Put in a layer of veal, sprinkle with salt, pepper, thyme, and anchovy or Worcestershire sauce, and then a layer of ham sprinkled with the egg. Fill the dish with alternate layers. Use both fat and lean of the ham. Cover and bake slowly 4 hours. When done, lay on it a heavy weight. Serve in thin slices.

Veal Collops.
Mrs. A. M., Milwaukee.

Cut part of a leg of veal into pieces 3 or 4 inches broad, sprinkle flour on them, fry in butter until brown, and then turn in water enough to cover the veal. When it boils take off the scum, put in 2 or 3 onions, a blade of mace, a little salt and pepper, and stew until tender; then take up the meat, thicken the gravy with flour and water mixed smoothly together, squeeze in the juice of a lemon—or a very good substitute is a teaspoonful of catsup—and turn the mixture over the brown collops. Garnish with thin slices of lemon.

Irish Stew.
Mrs. Frank G., Marquette.

Take lean mutton, potatoes and onions; first put in

a deep kettle a layer of potatoes cut in slices, then a layer of onions, then mutton, and be sure all the fat is cut off; then another layer of potatoes, onions and mutton; and finish by potatoes on top. Between each layer sprinkle salt, pepper and a little flour. Then put in enough water to cook without burning; cook 4 hours, and do not stir it up, but let it cook slowly on the top of the stove, with a hot fire, and it won't burn.

Mutton Dinner.
Mrs. M. E. M., Evanston.

Take 3 pounds of mutton, cut in small pieces,(if you skin mutton it loses the strong flavor), put it on the stove in cold water; when half done put in a teacup of rice. Pepper and salt to taste. Have water enough for soup. Make a nice biscuit crust, cut in diamonds, and 20 minutes before dinner drop them around on the top of the soup, and cover very closely; or steam if you prefer This, with a dish of nice potato salad and an apple pie, makes a very good though not a stylish dinner.

Pork Tenderloin.
Barry Grey, Chicago.

Cut the tenderloin open; stew in water till nearly done, then, with a little butter hissing in a spider, fry to a light brown—not too hard; have a small piece of toast buttered for each piece of meat; place the meat on the toast, pepper and salt, and then throw a thin milk gravy over all. We call it "quail on toast," and think it a very good substitute.

Baked Ham.
Busy Bee, Ottumwa, Iowa.

Make a crust of water and flour; roll half an inch thick; soak your ham over night and scrape well; then cover nice and tight with the crust, so the juice cannot escape, and bake it till done. Then remove all the crust and serve.

Boiled Ham.
Mrs. J. P. H., Chicago.

Clean thoroughly before cutting for any purpose. To boil, put in kettle of *cold water*, boil slowly till tender, and if intended to be eaten when cold, let it remain in the kettle just as it was cooked until cold.

Beef a la Mode.
Mrs. Sarah L., Chicago.

Buy a good roast—the tenderloin. Have the butcher put in a good piece of fat before he skewers it. Put in your ham boiler, or a kettle that can be hermetically (air tight) closed, an inch-thick slice of salt pork cut in small pieces, a pound of veal, a piece of butter, some salt, 2 or 3 cloves, some whole pepper, one onion cut in quarters, and one carrot quartered lengthwise. Lay the roast in, pour over a spoonful of vinegar, close and set over the fire; not too hot. In about 10 minutes add a cup of water, and turn the meat. In 15 another cup, and in 20 more another. Turn occasionally, but keep closed. Simmer slowly 4 hours. When done, carefully place upon a platter, putting a piece of carrot on each side, top and bottom. Turn all the grease out of the kettle, pour 2 tablespoonfuls of water into the kettle, give another boil, and turn over the meat.

Beef Stew.
G. M., Tiffin, Ohio.

In a stew-pan place a large tablespoonful of butter, in which fry until quite brown 2 sliced onions, adding while cooking 12 whole cloves; ditto allspice; $\frac{1}{4}$ a teaspoonful of salt, and $\frac{1}{2}$ that quantity of black pepper. Take from fire, pour in a pint of cold water, wherein lay 2 or 3 pounds of tender, lean beef cut in small, thick pieces. Cover closely, and let all stew gently 2 hours, adding just before serving a little flour thickening. A few sprigs of sweet basil is an improvement.

Beef Loaf.
X. Y. Z., Hudson, Mich.

$3\frac{1}{2}$ pounds of round steak chopped fine, 1 cup rolled crackers, 2 eggs, 1 cup milk, 1 teaspoon pepper, 1 tablespoon salt, piece of butter size of an egg. Bake $3\frac{1}{2}$ hours.

Meat Pie.
Mary Moore, Chicago.

In a 3-pint basin place a thick layer of stale bread, broken or chopped fine; on this a layer of boiled beef, sliced and seasoned with pepper and a pinch of powdered sage and parseley (the meat was salted enough when boiling); next a thick layer of bread again; then thoroughly moisten the whole with the broth of the beef, and bake half an hour in a moderate oven. The bottom of the pan should first be greased. 3 layers fill the pan full.

Veal Pot Pie.
Rizpah, Fon du Lac, Wis.

Cut in pieces 2 pounds of veal and boil in water until tender; season and add 6 potatoes sliced; boil until done and pour in a deep pan. Stir in a spoonful of flour and cover with a crust made like biscuit. Bake a light brown, but be sure to have plenty of gravy in the pie.

Veal Pie.
Sympathizer, Peoria, Ills.

Into 2 quarts of flour put teaspoonfuls of baking powder; sift, and add 1 teacupful of lard, wet up with $\frac{1}{2}$ pint of milk and $\frac{3}{4}$ of a pint of water; knead but little, roll out $\frac{1}{3}$ of the dough $\frac{1}{3}$ of an inch in thickness, and cut out the upper crust a little larger than the pan you bake in. (I use a pressed-tin milk-pan $12\frac{1}{4}$ inches in diameter and $3\frac{1}{2}$ deep, and this quantity for crust is just enough). With the rest of the dough line the pan, pressing it well up around the edge; bake 10 or 15 minutes. 2 hours before you make the crust, cut 3 or 4 pounds of veal into pieces less than 2 inches in thickness; those with bone (if any) should first be placed in the kettle, then the others, and cover with boiling water. As soon as the crust is the oven, season the veal, after removing the largest bones, with salt, pepper, and butter size of an egg; thicken with flour and milk, allowing gravy enough to cover the meat. When the undercrust is done, fill it with all of the meat, and all the gravy it will hold without running over, while you add the top crust; cut an opening in the center of this, and return to the oven for 15 or minutes, or until the upper crust is baked through and browned slightly. Send to the table in the pan to be carved there. An earthen dish is nicer, but they bake slower The rest of the gravy will be needed at the table.

Veal Cutlets.

Mrs. Sarah L., Chicago.

The way I cook cutlets and chops is to bake them. The great object is to have veal and mutton thoroughly cooked, and by baking you best accomplish that object. Take your dripping-pan, rub a little butter over each cutlet, salt and pepper, and lay flat in pans; place in hot oven, and cover with another pan of same size. When done, if you like, make a sauce called butter *maitre d'hotel.* Rub to a soft paste a small piece of butter with flour; pour over $\frac{1}{4}$ cup boiling hot water. It will then thicken; then add a teaspoonful of lemon-juice; pour over cutlets and serve. It's good for dinner.

Pork Chops.

Remove the skin, trim and dip in beaten egg, then in cracker-crumbs seasoned with salt, pepper, onion and sage. Fry in hot lard 20 minutes, turning often.

GAME

Broiled Quail.

Mrs. W. H. P., Peabody, Kansas.

EACH quail should be carefully picked, cut open down the back, and pounded slightly with the steak-pounder, to break the bones, so they will lie flat on the gridiron; salt and pepper them, and broil to a nice brown; have a pan of melted butter ready to dip each piece in as soon as cooked. Have ready slices of bread, toasted to a light brown, and well buttered. Lay a quail on each slice of the toast, then pour the butter which they were dipped in over the whole. Serve hot.

Wild Pigeons Stewed.

Emily W., Carondalet.

Clean and wash, then lay in salt water for an hour.

Rinse the inside with a solution of soda and water. Wash out with clear water, and stuff with bread and pork, chopped fine and seasoned. Sew up birds, and put on to cook in cold water sufficient to cover them, adding a slice of pork to each bird. Season to taste. Cook till tender; when done, place in a covered dish; strain the gravy, add juice of a lemon, a tablespoonful currant jelly, and thicken with flour; boil up, and pour over birds.

Roast Wild Duck.
Emily W., Carondalet.

Parboil 10 minutes, putting a carrot or onion in each; remove carrot or onion; lay in fresh water ½ hour; stuff with usual dressing; roast till brown and tender, basting with butter-water and drippings; to the gravy add tablespoon currant jell, and thicken with browned flour.

To Cook Venison.
Observer, Rock Springs, Wis.

Boil till tender, with sufficient water to keep from burning; when done put in some butter, pepper and salt; let it brown in the kettle; it retains all the flavor of the meat. That is the best way to cook roasts of beef; you then have juicy, tender meat.

Turkey Gravy.
Mrs. J. D. W., Chicago.

Heart, liver, gizzard and neck slashed and dredged thickly with flour. Put in a sauce pan with a little salt, a few peppercorns and allspice, and a little mace; outside skin of 3 onions, lump of butter the size of a walnut. When well browned, add boiling water till of proper thinness; let it cook slowly on the back part of the stove all the morning. After removing the turkey from the dripping-pan and pouring off any greese, put the prepared gravy into the dripping-pan, and proceed to make gravy same as any gravy.

Dressing for Poultry.
J. I. A., Dubuque.

Rub fine the soft part of a loaf of bread, add ½ a pound of butter, the yolks of 4 eggs, 1 teacup full of thyme or sweet marjoram; 1 tablespoonful black pepper; same of salt.

SHELL FISH.

Stewed Oysters.
Mrs. John B. D., Chicago.

PUT 1 quart of oysters into 3 quarts of boiling water, and pepper and salt to suit the taste. Leave the oysters in long enough to become heated through (as oysters should never be boiled). Then skim into the tureen. Now put in 1 pint of sweet cream, 12 crackers, and a good sized lump of butter, liquid. Let it come to a boil, and then pour into the tureen and send to the table.

Mrs. G. S., Rock River Falls.

To 1 can of oysters I allow 3 quarts of boiling water. I pour the boiling water over the oysters, and let the scum raise, and skim it off before seasoning. I then add ½ tea cup of sweet cream. Butter, salt and pepper to taste. Oysters take a great deal of salt. Let come to boil as quick as possible, *but do not boil.*

Delmonico's Stews.

The following is the formula used at the celebrated restaurants of Delmonico in New York, where, it is said, the finest oyster stews in the world are obtainable:

"Take 1 quart of liquid oysters, put the liquor (a teacupful for 3 persons) in a stew-pan, and add ½ as much more water; salt, a good bit of pepper, a teaspoonful of butter for each person, and a teaspoonful of rolled cracker for each. Put on the stove and let it boil; have the oysters ready in a bowl. The moment the liquor begins to boil pour in all the oysters, say 10 for each person. Now watch carefully, and as soon as it begins to boil, count just 30 seconds, and take the oysters from the stove. Have a big dish ready with 1½ tablespoonfuls of cold milk for each person. Pour the stew on this milk and serve immediately. Never boil an oyster if you wish it to be good."

Invalids' Oyster Soup.
Mrs. S. C. H., Chicago.

Procure the largest oysters; remove 6 from the can, 1 at a time, to a plate. Insert a fork into the solid flesh, and with a sharp knife make a slit up and down and across the abdominal cavity; slip the point of the knife under the dark mass thus exposed and thoroughly remove it, being as nice about it as you would in dressing any other fish, for the abdominal foulness of one is as unsuited to the stomach as the other. Put into stew-pan; pour out proper share of liquor, a pint of water and ½ gill of cream; add salt; pepper, if there be no fever; a teaspoonful of lemon juice, or 2 of pure cider vinegar. Bring just to the boil and pour into a dish. Break in cracker or nicely toasted thin slice of light bread. A little fresh butter makes it richer.

Escolloped Oysters.
Ivoline, Baltimore, Md.

To 2 quarts of fine oysters, 12 fresh crackers powdered fine, 1 cupful of oyster juice, 1 cupful of milk, a piece of butter the size of an egg, a little pepper and salt. Place alternate layers of oysters and crackers in a deep earthen dish, seasoning each layer of oysters with pepper and salt; when the dish is full, put the butter on top of the cracker crumbs, and pour the oyster juice and milk over all; set in a moderate oven and bake 50 minutes.

Jessie, Joliet, Ill.

First, lift your oysters from the liquor; then put in a deep dish, alternate layers o. rolled crackers and oysters, putting on each layer of oysters a little salt, pepper, and a little butter. Be sure and have your first and last layer consist of crackers. After you have the desired quantity in your dish, pour a sufficient amount of the liquor over the top to thoroughly moisten the crackers; put into a moderate oven and bake about 20 minutes.

Oyster Pie.
Busy Bee, Ottumwa, Iowa.

Make nice short biscuit crust; put a can of oysters, liquor and all, into a bright basin or yellow pudding pan; season with butter, salt and pepper; water if not a considerable quantity of liquor, for the crust soaks the liquor up; cover with a top crust—no bottom; bake quick, and serve hot. Cold sliced meats prepared the same way are very good.

Escolloped Oysters.
Shirley Dare, Bryan, Ohio.

Crush the desired quantity of crackers; put a layer in the bottom of a buttered dish; wet this with a mixture of the oyster-liquor and milk slightly warm; next a layer of oysters; sprinkle them with salt and pepper, and lay bits of butter upon them; then another layer of moistened crumbs, and so on. Let the top layer be of crumbs thicker than the rest, and beat an egg in the milk poured over them. Stick bits of butter thickly over it; cover the dish, and bake 40 minutes; remove the cover and brown by setting it on the upper grate of the oven for a few minutes.

Cream Oysters. On the Half-Shell.

Pour into a pan 1 cup of hot water, 1 cup milk, and 1 of cream (or 3 cupfuls of milk). Set it in a kettle of hot water until it boils; stir in 2 tablespoonfuls of butter, and pepper and salt to suit; take from the fire and stir in 2 heaping tablespoonfuls of corn-starch, wet up in cold milk. Have the shells cleaned and buttered and laid in a baking-pan; place an oyster in each shell; stir the cream hard and fill carefully; bake 5 or 6 minutes after the shells are warm. If shells are not easily obtained, patty-pans or small sauce-dishes answer every purpose. Serve in the shell or dishes.

Fried Oysters.

Dip each oyster in beaten egg; then in rolled cracker or corn-meal, and fry quickly in hot butter.

Oyster Sauce.
Louise, Chicago.

Take 12 good oysters, 6 ounces good melted butter, a little red pepper, 3 tablespoons of cream. Stir all together over a slow fire, bring to a boil, and then serve.

Chowder.
Little Rhody, Aurora, Ill.

Take 4 or 5 slices of salt pork, fry in the spider a

delicate brown; remove, and cut in pieces; then in the pork fat fry 3 or 4 good-sized onions sliced thin; have ready 12 potatoes, pared and sliced, also 4 or 5 cakes of hard bread; put the hard bread to soak (whole) in some cold water; then take the soup-kettle and put first a layer of pork, then of onions, next of potatoes, and finally of clams or fish, as the case may be, and so on alternately, seasoning highly with pepper and salt; and lastly, putting a layer of the soaked hard bread on top; first cover with water and boil 20 minutes.

Octavia, Amboy, Ill.

For a can of clams, pare and cut in thin slices potatoes to nearly fill a quart measure; put 3 or 4 thin slices of nice salt pork in the kettle in which the chowder is to be cooked; when the pork is about half fried, put a layer of the sliced potatoes over the pork, then a layer of clams, then a layer of Boston crackers which have been split open and slightly buttered and dipped quickly in cold water; then potatoes, clams, and crackers again, until all is in the kettle. Now sprinkle over a little salt and pepper, and afterwards pour on milk, or, if milk is not plenty, milk and water, to just cover the whole. Let boil very gently, closely covered, without stirring, for about half an hour, or until the potatoes are done. Then remove carefully to a tureen for the table. The pork prevents the mass from sticking to the kettle, and helps to season the chowder. Fresh fish chowder made in this way, with milk, is delicious.

Myrtle, Chicago.

Clam or fish : 1 quart water; 2 slices pork; 2 ordinary-sized onions, sliced thin. Boil 20 minutes; add 6 quartered potatoes; 1 pound halibut laid on the top; put in butter, pepper and salt to taste—the higher seasoned the better; thicken with a little flour; stew ½ an hour. Just before taking up put in a pint of oyster crackers, and you have a genuine chowder, a la seaside.

SALADS.

Chicken Salad.
Ella, Chicago.

TAKE the breasts of 2 chickens; 2 large bunches of celery and 4 hard-boiled eggs; chop these separately and fine; put together and mix thoroughly. Then make a gravy of 1 tablespoonful of mustard; 2 tablespoonfuls of sugar; 1 cup of vinegar; and ½ cup of butter; pour hot over the salad.

Mary, Chicago.

Boil a chicken, seasoned in cooking, until it parts readily from the bone; pour off the liquor. When the fowl is cold, pick it from the bones and chop fine in a wooden bowl. Use the same quantity of celery or cabbage cut with a knife and the chopped whites of 2 hard-boiled eggs. Mix, and put away until within an hour of using, when the following previously-prepared dressing must be mixed with it: Beat the yolks and whites of 2 eggs separately; into that stir 3 tablespoonfuls of melted butter or table oil; 1½ teaspoons of salt; 2 teaspoons of celery salt or seed; 1 tablespoon of hard butter, and ⅔ of a teacup of vinegar. Cook in an earthen or new tin dish until as thick as pound-cake. When cold, add ⅔ of a teacup of sweet milk or cream.

Potato Salad.
C. L. D. B., Chicago.

Take medium-sized potatoes; boil; let them get cold; then slice them; put in a medium-sized onion, chopped fine; take a teacup ⅔ full of best cider-vinegar, into which put a tablespoonful of sweet oil; heat the vinegar and oil very hot; pour over the potatoes and onions, and stir all together with a salad spoon; then let it get cold, and you have a fine potato salad.

Bean Salad.
M. L. H., Elgin, Ill.

Cover the bottom of your salad-dish with cold boiled potatoes, sliced thin; over this spread a layer of cold baked (or boiled) beans, and above this a layer of onions, sliced very thin; salt and pepper each layer; heat a piece of butter the size of a walnut in sufficient vinegar to cover the salad, and pour over it while hot.

Cabbage Salad.
Mrs. Gen. W., Chicago.

Take 1 head of nice cabbage and chop very fine with salt, after which set it away for a few days. Then drain off all the water, and add 1 tablespoon of mustard seed, and enough vinegar to cover, and boil it $\frac{1}{2}$ hour. This is to be eaten cold.

Lobster Salad.
Winnie, Charleston.

Boil a hen lobster; when done remove the meat from the shell; mince it; rub the coral to a smooth paste with a tablespoon of olive oil or melted butter; add the grated yolks of 3 hard-boiled eggs; 1 teaspoon of mustard; salt and pepper to taste; a wine-glass of good cider vinegar; mix the sauce with the meat; add a third as much with lettuce or celery, cut fine, just before serving. Salmon salad may be made the same way, garnished with lemon, sliced thin, and parseley or celery.

Cream Salad.
Marion, Racine, Wis.

Chop fine $\frac{1}{2}$ a head of cabbage; into it stir a little salt and $\frac{1}{2}$ a cup of thick cream; heat $\frac{1}{2}$ a cup of vinegar, stirring into it the beaten yolks of 2 eggs, a teaspoonful of sugar, and $\frac{1}{2}$ a teaspoonful of mustard; pour this over the cabbage just as it goes to the table.

Cabbage Salad.
Busy Bee, Ottumwa, Iowa.

Two eggs, 2 tablespoonfuls of sugar, 1 of butter, $\frac{1}{2}$ cup sweet milk well beaten, with a little salt and pepper, stir into one pint of boiling vinegar, and keep stirring till it boils again; then cool and pour over very fine sliced cabbage.

VEGETABLES.

Potato Puff.
Eloise Howe, Rockford, Ill.

TWO cups cold mashed potatoes; bits of some kind of cold meat hashed; 2 tablespoons melted butter; 2 well-beaten eggs; 1 cup milk; pour into a deep dish and bake in a quick oven; if rightly done, will merit its name.

Busy Bee, Ottumwa, Iowa.

Take cold beef or lean meat of any kind; cut in small bits; season with salt and pepper; boil and mash some potatoes; make into paste with 1 or 2 eggs; roll out with a dust of flour; cut with a saucer; put the cut-meat on $\frac{1}{2}$ of crust; fold the other over, and pinch together; fry brown in butter.

Potatoes a la Creme.
Mrs. E. D. G, H., Grand Rapids, Mich.

Put into a saucepan 2 ounces butter, a dessertspoonful of flour, some parseley and scallions (both chopped small), salt and pepper. Stir them together; add a wineglass of cream, and set on the stove, stirring constantly until it boils. Cut some boiled potatoes into slices and put into the pan with the mixture, and boil all together, and serve *very hot*.

Steamed Potatoes.
Mrs. Sarah L., Chicago.

Steam or boil dry a quart of sound potatoes; then peel and mash in a sauce-pan, and mix an ounce of butter; set over the fire, pouring in slowly nearly $\frac{1}{2}$ a pint of milk; stir to prevent scorching; dish into a common earthen dish, scollop and put in quick oven to brown; set on table in same dish. This is the most palatable way of cooking potatoes, especially in the spring.

COOKERY—VEGETABLES.

Fancy Mashed Potatoes.
Mrs. H. Frank B., Chicago.

Peel 2 quarts potatoes, and when they are cooked, turn off every drop of water, put in a little salt, pepper and butter; then take a carving-fork and break them up a little; next add a little more butter, say, in the whole, a piece as large as an egg, and nearly a cup of nice milk or cream. Now take a silver fork, or 3-pronged one, and beat them briskly 5 minutes, or until light and creamy. They must be carried immediately to the table, or they will become heavy and clammy. If once tried this way you will never again resort to the old " masher." Remember, they must be served immediately.

To Boil.
Marian Warren, Chicago.

In boiling potatoes, when they are not previously pared, always have a ring of the skin a $\frac{1}{4}$ of an inch peeled from end to end. This is not a " notion," but the escape of the water, and consequently the mealiness of the potato, is very much promoted by it. It does no harm to cut large potatoes in halves or quarters before boiling.

Fried Potatoes.
Mrs. D. S. F., Rockford.

Peel, then slice rather thin into cold water. If very thin, they may be too crisp. Let them stand in the water a short time, and then drain through a colander; have ready on the stove a kettle of hot lard, as for fried cakes; put in part of the potatoes and cover the kettle; stir them occasionally; when done they should be a delicate brown; skim out into any dish, and sprinkle a little salt over them. When the second batch of potatoes is partly cooked, let me advise you to ring your bell, as they will be cooked by the time the first lot is disposed of, and are much better hot.

Boiled-Baked Sweet Potatoes.
Nannie C., Lake View.

Boil your potatoes until tender; then slice several times the long way of the potato; place a layer of the slices on the bottom of an earthen dish; sprinkle lightly with white sugar, and heavily with lumps of butter (it is the butter that makes it nice); then another layer of potatoes, and so on, until you have the sugar and butter for a top layer; then bake 30 or 40 minutes.

Egg Plant.
Mrs. Enos, Evansville, Ind.

To cook egg-plant, slice the plant ¼ inch thick; sprinkle with salt; place layer upon layer, and let stand 15 minutes; dip in a batter and fry in butter and lard. Another good way is to dip in egg and roll in crushed cracker and fry same way.

Corn Oysters.
M. H., Chicago.

Six ears of sweet corn (those which are not too old); with a sharp knife split each row of the corn in the center of the kernel lengthwise; scrape out all the pulp; add 1 egg, well beaten, a little salt, 1 tablespoonful of sweet milk; flour enough to make a pretty stiff batter; drop in hot lard, and fry a delicate brown. If the corn is quite young, omit the milk, using as little flour as possible.

Asparagus.
Mrs. Sarah L., Chicago.

Scrape. Put in water and salt, and at first boil; drop in the asparagus; boil till tender. Sauce: 1 yolk of egg mixed with a teaspoonful of water; a piece of butter added, and when hot, stir in 2 tablespoonfuls of milk; pour over the drained asparagus.

Baked Beans.
Mrs. E., Kalamazoo.

Take as many beans as you think you want; wash, boil till tender, and add salt, pepper, and molasses to taste. If you like them greasy, put in " right smart " of pork; a small piece will answer. Bake in covered dish of any sort.

Boston Baked Beans.
Mrs. H. V. R., Chicago.

Wash; then par-boil ½ an hour; then bake all day or night. As to the seasoning, it is much a matter of taste. Some like them with a good deal of fat, and into a pot that would hold a quart of beans, would put ¼ a pound of pork (salt), cutting through the rind as if to slice, then laying it at the top, so that the rind may become nicely brown. Then some add a tablespoonful of molasses. We do not believe much in pork, so only put in a very thin slice of it. adding a little salt and omitting the sweetening.

D. S., *Belvidere, Ill.*

Take 1 pint of beans and let them soak over night in a quart of cold water; in the morning pour the water off, and let them stand about an hour in fresh water on top of the stove, and then remove to a regular " Boston bean-pot," not a common yellow dish, as half of the western people do, and lay ¼ a pound of salt pork (not too fat) across the top of them and 2 tablespoonfuls of New Orleans molasses, and cover all with water, and put in the oven, and let them bake until the middle of the afternoon, during the day adding water as it cooks away; and for Sunday morning's breakfast set the bean-pot in the oven again (with your beans undisturbed from the night before), and add a cup of hot water, and let them remain about an hour, and you will find them delicious. Serve with a loaf of brown bread, and you can imagine yourself eating a Boston breakfast. I make a sweet sauce from ripe tomatoes, which eaten upon beans, gives them a great relish. I advise those who never tried it, for meats or beans. to immediately make a large jar full for winter.

Baked Beans.
Mrs. H. Frank B., Chicago.

For a family of 4 or 5, take 1 quart of beans, the smaller the better, and soak them 10 or 12 hours; then put in 1 pound of salt pork, not too lean; put them in a deep jar or " crock," and sink the pork in the beans all but the rind. which must be scored, or gashed, about ½ an inch apart; cover the whole with the water the beans were soaked in; if not enough, add more cold water, a little salt and pepper, and bake 10 or 12 hours. I put mine in the oven at 6 p. m., and cook them all night with a slow fire. Some put in a tablespoonful of molasses. This will make 2 good meals, and the more they are warmed over the better they are.

Fried Tomatoes.

Take large green tomatoes; cut off both ends, and then cut up 1 in 3 slices. Have some butter in the frying-pan; let it get hot; then roll the tomatoes in flour and lay them in the pan; salt, pepper, and sprinkle a little sugar on while frying; cook till they are done nice and brown, and you will have a most delicious article for breakfast.

Egg Plant.
Mrs. T. G. E., Chicago.

Cut slices ½ an inch thick, and pare, when first starting breakfast. Rub salt lightly over the top of each slice and let stand in a pile till the brine starts; then shake off the salt and dip each slice, both sides, into flour well, stand in a pile till the flour is moist, then fry in a little lard in the frying-pan, like one would griddle-cakes. When brown, take up and spread a little butter on top of each slice.

Cooking Egg Plant.
Mrs. C. G. S., Chicago.

To cook egg plant—Slice and leave in salt water a short time before using; dip in beaten egg; after, in corn-meal or cracker crumbs; fry brown in butter and lard.

To Cook Dry Peas.
Kit, Crete, Neb.

Choose the green, wrinkled peas; soak a pint of them over night; set them on the stove early in the morning with cold water enough to cover them well; simmer very gently, adding cold water as they evaporate. Do not let them boil, and they will come to the table whole and sound. Do not salt until they are done, and they will be as tender as June peas. A little butter is all the dressing they will need.

Hominy Fritters.
E. L. M., Chicago.

Two teacupfuls of cold boiled hominy; stir in 1 teacupful of sweet milk and a little salt, 4 tablespoonfuls of sifted flour and 1 egg. Beat the white separately and add last. Have over the fire a pan of hot lard; drop the batter in by spoonfuls, and fry a nice brown. This is especially designed for a breakfast side dish, and rice is good used in place of the hominy.

Boiled Hominy.
E. L. M., Chicago.

Boiled: Soak 1 cup of fine hominy in 3 cups of water, with salt to taste. In the morning turn it into a quart pail, then put the pail into a kettle of boiling water, cover tightly, and steam 1 hour; then add 1 teacup of sweet milk, and boil 15 minutes after stirring the milk in.

Hulled Corn.
F. S. P., Moline.

Take 3 quarts corn, 3 quarts unleeched wood ashes (or ¼ pound potash); to ashes or potash add 6 quarts water, which boil and skim; strain lye into kettle; put in the corn; boil until skins break from kernels easily, stirring frequently; skim out the corn, rinse it several times, rubbing thoroughly last time; leave it to soak in clear water 10 minutes, when rub off black chits; rinse again; put back into kettle, cover with water, boil slowly till soft; keep hot water to add until boiled tender; salt. Eat with cream and sugar.

"Domin Nopinee."

Take a ½ pint of yellow corn; roast it like coffee over a slow fire; clean out the coffee-mill; grind 1 coarse, 1 fine; eat with milk and a little salt, after it has stood 5 or 10 minutes to swell.

Succotash.
Aunt Eliza, Andover, Ct.

Take 1 quart Lima beans, ½ pound pork, 1½ dozen ears sweet corn (green); boil the pork 1½ hours in 3 quarts of water, putting in the beans when the pork has boiled ½ an hour. Cut the corn off, putting it in 1 dish; into another scrape the milk from the cobs. When the beans are nearly done, put in the corn, and boil 15 minutes; then add the milk from the cobs, boiling all 10 minutes longer. It should be a little thicker than gruel. Stir all the time after adding the milk, or it will burn. If not sweet enough, add sugar.

Scolloped Tomatoes.

Peel, slice and pack in a pudding dish in alternate layers, with a thick layer of bread crumbs mixed with butter, salt, pepper and a little white sugar. When the dish is nearly full, put tomatoes uppermost; lay a piece of butter on each slice; dust with pepper, salt and sugar; cover lightly with crumbs and bake covered ¼ an hour; remove lid and bake brown.

Boiled Cabbage.
Jennie June.

Strip off the outside leaves; cut in quarters, and lay for an hour in cold water; cover with boiling water and cook 15 minutes; turn off the water and cover with fresh boiling water; cook until tender, perhaps an hour; drain well; chop and stir in a tablespoonful of butter, pepper and salt. Serve hot. Some prefer to boil a piece of pork with the cabbage. It will give a delicious flavor.

Baked Cabbage.

Cook as for boiled cabbage, after which drain and set aside until cold. Chop fine, add 2 beaten eggs, a tablespoon of butter, pepper, salt, 3 tablespoons rich cream; stir well, and bake in a buttered dish until brown. Eat hot.

Green Peas.

Shell and lay in cold water for an hour; put into salted boiling water and cook ½ an hour. Drain well, and season with butter and pepper.

Baked Onions.

Wash, but do not peel the onions; boil 1 hour in boiling water, slightly salt, changing the water twice in the time. When tender, drain on a cloth and roll each in buttered tissue paper, twisted at the top, and bake an hour in a slow oven. Peel and brown them. Serve with melted butter.

Browned Potatoes.

Boil; and ¾ of an hour before a roast of beef is

taken from the oven, put them in the dripping-pan, after skimming off the fat from the gravy; baste them frequently, and when quite brown drain on a sieve.

Mashed Turnips.

Pare and lay in cold water, slightly salted, 10 minutes; cook with boiling water, and cook until very tender; drain and wash in a collander; season with butter, pepper and salt. Serve hot.

Escolloped Onions.
Miss Lee Any, Alton, Ill.

Boil till tender 6 large onions. Afterwards separate them with a large spoon; then place a layer of onions and a layer of grated bread crumbs alternately in a pudding dish. Season with pepper and salt to taste; moisten with milk; put in the oven to brown.

Cracked Wheat.
Small Housekeeper, at Home.

Stir 5 large heaping spoonfuls of the crushed white wheat sold by grocers into a quart of boiling water, and set the tin pail holding it into a pan of boiling water to cook 20 minutes. This prevents its burning, and is a cheap and easy substitute for a farina kettle. Salt well, and when the kernels have swelled and burst like popcorn it is done. Serve it plain to eat with meat and gravy like rice, or add $\frac{1}{4}$ a teaspoonful of cinnamon, a pinch of ground cloves, a handful of raisins or currants, and a $\frac{1}{2}$ cup of sugar while boiling, and you have a savory breakfast dish. Sometimes we serve it plain in saucers, with a dust of cinnamon on the top, and sugar and butter or cream, as German pancake is eaten.

EGGS.

Boiling Eggs.
Jennie Lee, Chicago.

PUT the eggs in some vessel which can be closely covered, and when the tea-kettle boils pour in water enough to cover them, close the vessel and place it on the back part of the stove, and let it remain 10 minutes. If you wish to be very exact, use a thermometer and keep the water 10 minutes at exactly the heat which is indicated after the water is poured in.

By the ordinary method of letting the eggs boil from 2 to 4 minutes the white part is hardened and the yolk left uncooked, or if the yolk is cooked the white is too hard. By this method the heat penetrates so gradually that the yolk is nicely cooked, while the white is soft and tender and only just done enough to be opaque.

Poached Eggs.
Mrs. W. S. D., Lowell.

Place a frying-pan of salted boiling water on the fire filled with as many small muffin-rings as it will hold; break the eggs singly in a cup and pour into the rings; boil them 2½ or 3 minutes; remove the rings and take up the eggs singly in a strainer; serve on ½ slices of nicely browned and buttered toast; put a small piece of butter on each egg; pepper slightly, and garnish with sprigs of parsley. Serve hot.

Omelet.
Gypsy, Ionia, Mich.

Take six eggs and beat separately; allow one tablespoonful of milk to each egg; stir in flour to make a batter; take a cupful of milk, put on the stove, and stir in the batter until it is like starch; add a piece of butter the size of a walnut and a pinch of salt; take this from the stove; pour into the dish in which you would serve; then stir in the yolks of the eggs, which have been beaten; beat the whites until you can turn the platter bottom side up; then add them, mixing thoroughly; put in a quick oven and bake 10 minutes. Should be eaten immediately.

Annie M. Hale, M. D., Chicago.

Break 6 eggs into a bowl. Skim out the yolks into a large coffee-cup. Beat the whites to a stiff froth. Now beat the yolks enough to make them smooth, fill up the cup with milk and pour this into the bowl containing the whites of the eggs. Put in a little salt and stir enough to mix the whole—that is, as little as possible. Have the spider warmed and a piece of butter as large as an egg already melted therein. Now pour in your eggs and milk, let it cook slowly; be sure and not burn. If there is danger of this lift it up from the bottom with a knife. When the froth *sets* on the top it is done. Put a large plate over the spider and deftly turn the whole upside down. Lift off the spider and you will have an elegant and delicious omelet.

Jane B., Waukegan.

Take 1 egg for each person, beat 2 minutes, add salt the size of a pea and 1 tablespoonful of milk for each egg; beat 1 minute and turn into a hot, well-buttered frying-pan; cover it and cook slowly till nearly as thick; raise the edges and put under a little butter or lard to prevent sticking, and turn 1 half over on the other half, and serve immediately.

French Eggs.
Roxey, No. 2, Chicago.

Boil hard, remove the shells, and roll in cracker crumbs; fry in butter until brown. Make a gravy of butter, crumbs and cream, and pour over them.

Pickled Eggs.
Algebra, Chicago.

Select nine fresh ones, boil them hard, lift them directly from the hot water into cold. When cool, remove the shell, stick cloves into them, and drop in cold vinegar.

Agnes, Chicago.

Put the eggs on the stove in cold water, let stand and boil for 1 hour—the heart is then mealy; remove the shells, stick 4 or 5 cloves in each egg, pour hot vinegar over (add other spices if you like); let stand a few days; they are very nice.

To Keep Eggs.
Mrs. C. G. S., Rock River Valley.

Pour one gallon of boiling water on one quart of quicklime. When cold, add one ounce cream tartar. The eggs must be covered with the pickle.

Fancier, Chicago.

Take any tight package and place a layer of fine salt over the bottom; into this set the eggs, large end down, as closely as possible without touching each other; fill with salt until the layer is covered, and then proceed as before. Care must be taken that the salt is dry, and that it be kept so, else it will cake and make it very troublesome to get the eggs out without breaking.

French Toast.
Belle, Chicago.

For dessert: ⅔ of a pint of milk; 1 egg, well beaten; a little salt. Take 6 slices of bread; dip into the custard (uncooked) 1 by 1; then fry in a little butter till a delicate brown. For sauce, melted sugar with a little cinnamon added. This is very nice, and is a good way to use up stale bread.

P. P. C., Chicago.

Beat 3 or 4 eggs; season with salt and pepper; have ready some thin slices of bread; dip them into the eggs, and fry them in lard (or after frying ham) until of a light brown.

Another method of cooking eggs and bread together is to crumb the bread some, as for dressing; mix it with 3 or 4 beaten eggs; season, and fry until thoroughly done; or mold with the hands into cakes, and fry until of a light brown. Either of the above dishes form a pleasant addition to the morning's repast.

COFFEE.

A Woman, New Boston, Ill.

MAKE the best green coffee, roast to a dark-brown, beat the white of 1 egg (so it won't hang together much), stir it through the coffee while hot. When sufficiently browned, put away in a close can while hot. Grind when you want to make your coffee enough for a tablespoon heaping full to each person; add as many cups cold water as you think your family will drink; put in a hot place; let it just come to a boil; put it back where it will keep hot till your meal is ready; then put it off the stove 2 or 3 minutes before pouring out. If not strong enough, put in more coffee next time.

Mrs. F. C. E., Burlington, Iowa.

A recipe for making coffee which has been used in my family for 75 years: Buy the green berry; brown and grind it at home; grind as fine as mill will grind it. Buy a French biggin—dimensions of top portion to make coffee for 1 person—1⅜ inches in diameter, 5 inches high; for 2 or 3 persons, 2¼ inches diameter, 4 to 5 inches high. Quantity of unground coffee for 1 person, contents of a tin cup 1¾ inches in diameter, 1½ inches deep; for two persons, 1¾ inches in diameter, 2 inches deep. Put the coffee into the top of the pot, with nothing between it and the perforated bottom; press it tight; put in the strainer. (This is to prevent the water from striking the coffee in a body, thus boring a hole in it, and running through without extracting its strength). Pour in boiling water ¼ of a pint at a time, allowing ¼ of a pint for each person, and ¼ of a pint for absorption. (Where there are more than 3 persons, allow more for absorption; where fewer, less). While water is running through, the bottom pot or receiver should stand in hot water. (This prevents boiling or getting cold). This coffee should always be used with hot milk—proportion, 1 part coffee, 3 parts milk.

Lillie W., Englewood, Ills.

Take 2 or more egg-shells, crush them with the requisite amount of ground Java, add ¼ a cup of cold water, beat it well together, pour on boiling water, and allow it to boil up once. Always wash eggs before breaking them, and save the shells for coffee, which will be, when so treated, as clear as when the white of an egg is used.

Aunt Sally, Springfield, O.

Take a piece of Shaker flannel, and make a bag that will fit in your coffee-pot, only make it about an inch shorter. Hem in a piece of wire or hoop-skirt steel, just below the hem at the top (something to hold the bag up), and put a loop on. Hang this bag in the coffee-pot, and put the coffee in the bag, pour in the boiling water, a pint to a heaping tablespoonful of coffee, and boil. You will have nice clear coffee, without using eggs or anything else to clear it.

Mrs. Lillian D. Bollam, Chicago.

Roast to a brown color (don't *burn* to a black) *genuine* Mocha or old Government Java; grind while yet warm; place the quantity required for breakfast, loose (not packed), in a thin muslin sack; drop this sack to the bottom of the coffee-pot; fill the pot with cold water; place it on the stove until it gradually reaches the boiling heat, *but don't let it boil for an instant;* keep the pot on the stove 10 minutes longer, and the strength will be drawn from the ground coffee. Pour the coffee into *warm* cups directly from the pot. Add *warm* cream or *hot* milk, and sugar, and you will have an exquisite draught, all things having been properly conducted, equal to the fabled nectar we read of in mythology. Roast coffee every morning—use as soon as roasted.

D. D. Chicago.

One-half egg to 1 cup ground coffee; stir well in a bowl, so that every ground is covered; then place in the coffee-pot and pour on cold water—shaking constantly till the lump of egg and coffee settles to a smooth mass. Add your boiling water.

Mrs. Evergreen City, Bloomington.

For each person allow 1 tablespoonful of coffee; pour on boiling water sufficient for use; boil from 3 to 5 minutes, after which pour out ½ a cupful and replace it in the pot, allowing it to stand about a minute—this settles the coffee nicely—when it is ready to serve.

Buelah, Ottawa, Ill.

Boil a dessert-spoonful of ground coffee in a pint of milk for a ¼ of an hour; then clear it with white of egg or isinglass; let it boil for a few minutes, and set it by the side of the fire to fine. Sweeten according to taste. This is a suitable breakfast for those of spare habit and disposed to affections of the lungs.

Queechy, DesPlaines, Ills.

You can make coffee perfectly clear by putting in a small piece of codfish-skin, about 5 minutes before it is taken from the stove. A piece an inch square will be sufficient for a good sized family. The outside should be scraped, then rinse it and drop it in.

Mrs. Nellie Townsend, Chicago.

In the first place get the green coffee, roast it, take the quantity required, put in coffee-pot, pour boiling water on it; have a pot of boiling water, set in this the coffee-pot, with a small piece of wood for the coffee-pot to rest on, so it will not touch the bottom of the pot; let it boil a half-hour, or, for that matter, it might boil all day, and be all the better for it. Your coffee will be as clear as crystal. You will need no egg, and will also find you will not require as much coffee as boiling. This way does not boil but steeps it. Be careful to use boiling water for both.

B. Frank, Peoria.

Get the best of green coffee, and brown nicely, but be sure and not burn it; and while it is cooling, take the whites of 3 eggs and beat them until they are slightly frothy, and while the coffee is warm pour them over and stir well together, and when well mixed, if it should not be dry, set the pan under the stove to dry. Grind a cupful of the coffee, and to every person put a heaping tablespoonful of the coffee in a coffee-pot. Then pour a cup of cold water over it and shake well;

set it on the stove; let it come to a boil, and put in as many cups of boiling water as you have spoonfuls of coffee; stir down the grounds from the sides of the coffee-pot; pour in a little cold water; let it stand a little while and it is ready to serve.

BREAD.

Puffett.
R., Dubuque, Iowa.

1 quart sifted flour, in which rub 2 teaspoons cream tartar; butter, size of an egg; 2 teaspoons powdered sugar, 2 eggs beaten; mix very smooth and add 1 pint milk and 1 teaspoon soda dissolved in a little boiling water. Bake immediately.

Muffins.
Critic, Chicago.

1 quart flour; three teaspoonfuls baking-powder, or 2 heaping teaspoonfuls of cream tartar (which I prefer), and one rounding full of soda, both stirred in the flour; ⅞ of a cup of butter, or lard, or half and half; put on the stove to melt without getting hot; beat 2 eggs in a bowl; add a little less than a pint of milk; stir into the flour a little salt; add the butter last; have irons quite hot and fill even full; then bake.

Mrs. E. D. T. H., Grand Rapids, Mich.

1 quart of rich milk, or, ½ cream and ½ milk; 1 quart of flour—heaping; 6 eggs; 1 tablespoonful of butter, and 1 of lard, softened together. Beat whites and yolks separately, very light. Then add flour and shortening, and a scant teaspoonful of salt, and stir in the flour the last thing, lightly as possible, and have the butter free from lumps. Heat your muffin rings, butter well, and half fill them, and bake immediately in hot oven. Send them to the table the moment they are done.

R., *Dubuque, Iowa.*

1 pint sweet milk; 3 eggs; 2 tablespoons melted butter; 1 teaspoon soda; 2 teaspoons cream tartar; batter as stiff as for buckwheat cakes.

Mrs. Sarah L., *Chicago.*

1 cup milk; 2 eggs; ⅔ cup lard; salt; 1 teaspoonful baking powder. Make a batter not too stiff, and bake in gem-tins; 15 or 20 minutes will do.

Quick Muffins.
Henrietta, *Warsaw, Ind.*

1 cup milk; 1 cup flour; 1 egg, well beaten, salt. Have your gem-irons very hot; fill ½ full and bake quickly. These are delicious with good butter and maple sirup.

Corn Meal Muffins.
Cousin Nell, *Chicago.*

1½ cups of corn-meal; the same of flour; 2 teaspoons of baking-powder; ½ cup of sugar; ¼ teaspoon of salt; small tablespoon of melted butter; 2 eggs; milk enough to make a stiff batter.

Drop Biscuits.
Aunt Sally, *Springfield, O.*

1 quart of flour; 3 teaspoonsful of baking powder; 1 small teaspoonful of salt; piece of butter the size of an egg, rubbed thoroughly in the flour; 1 pint of milk; dropped from a spoon in buttered pans; bake in a quick oven.

Soda Biscuits.
Mrs. Beal, *Dixon.*

3 pints of flour, a tablespoon of butter and do. lard, a teaspoon of salt, do. even full cream of tartar, 1 of soda; sift the cream tartar with the flour dry, rub the butter and lard very thoroughly through it; dissolve the soda in a pint of milk, and mix all together. Roll out, adding as little flour as possible; cut with a biscuit-cutter, and bake 20 minutes in a quick oven.

Yeast Biscuit.
Gwendolen, *Monzomania, Wis.*

2 quarts of flour, 1 tablespoonful of butter; 3 table-

spoonsful of sugar; ¼ cup yeast; a little salt. Mix thoroughly with 1 pint of scalded milk when it is almost cold. This will seem hard, but when raised will mold easily. Mix at night and mold in the morning. Cut out and let them stand until raised again; then bake.

Baking-Powder Biscuit.
Mrs. O. H. H., Chicago.

One important point is in having a *hot oven;* another is, have flour sifted, and roll dough as soft as you can handle; then more baking-powder is needed. For each teacup of flour take a teaspoon of powder; butter, the size of a small hen's egg, is sufficient for a quart of flour. After rubbing butter and powder into the amount of flour needed, I turn in cold water (milk will do), stirring all of the time, till the right consistency is reached; salt; then roll lightly, and bake at once. I warrant these will prove flakey, feathery, delicious, and more nutritious than biscuit raised with yeast.

Mrs. G. Clinton Smith, Springfield, Ills.

Use 3 heaping teaspoons baking powder. Rub this with your hands—not a spoon—into a quart of flour thoroughly. Then rub in a heaping tablespoonful of butter or lard in the same manner you did the baking-powder until well mixed. After adding a teaspoon of salt, if lard is used, add milk or water sufficient to make a soft dough. Roll and cut out quickly, placing them at once in a very hot oven. This latter is important. Unless the oven is very hot they will not be a success.

Quick Biscuits.
Mrs. Emily, Eau Claire, Wis.

Mix a quart of sweet milk with ½ a cup melted butter; stir in a pinch of salt, 2 teaspoonfuls baking-powder, and flour enough for a stiff batter. Have the oven at a brisk heat. Drop the batter, a spoonful in a place, on buttered pans. They will bake in 15 minutes.

Graham Biscuits.
Mrs. J. H. H., Moline.

Take 1 quart water or milk, butter the size of 1 egg, 3 tablespoonfuls sugar, 2 of baker's yeast, and a pinch of salt. Take enough white flour to use up the water, making it the consistency of batter cakes. Add the rest of the ingredients, and as much Graham flour as can be stirred in with a spoon. Set it away till morning. In the morning grease pan, flour hands. Take a lump dough the size of a large egg; roll lightly between the palms. Let them rise 20 minutes, and bake in a tolerably hot oven.

Rusks.
Mrs. W. F., Tuscola, Ills.

Take enough of light dough and work in a teacup of sugar and nearly as much shortening, mould out same as for light biscuit. Or, take a teacupful of yeast, $\frac{1}{2}$ a cup of lard or butter, a little soda; knead together, and when it rises mold out, and raise again before baking.

May Ely, Rochester.

Rusks require a longer time for rising than ordinary rolls or biscuits. If wished for tea one evening, begin them the day before. In cold weather, to make up $2\frac{1}{4}$ quarts of flour, mix into a paste with one pint of boiling water, 2 tablespoonfuls of sugar, 3 of flour, and 2 large Irish potatoes, boiled and mashed smooth. In the evening make up dough with this sponge, adding 3 well beaten eggs, $\frac{3}{4}$ of a pound sugar, and $\frac{1}{2}$ a pint fresh milk. Set it away in a covered vessel, leaving plenty of room for it to swell. Next morning work into the risen dough, which should not be stiff, a $\frac{1}{4}$ pound of butter and lard mixed. Make into rolls or biscuits, and let the dough rise for the second time. Flavor with 2 grated nutmegs or $\frac{1}{4}$ an ounce of pounded stick cinnamon. When very light, bake in a quick, steady oven till of a pretty brown color; glaze with the yolk of an egg, and sprinkle lightly with powdered white sugar.

Spanish Buns.
H. A. H., Oshkosh, Wis.

One pint of flour; 1 pint sugar; 1 cup sweet milk; 1 cup of butter; 4 eggs, beat separate; 1 tablespoon of cinnamon; 1 teaspoon cloves; 1 teaspoon of soda; 2 teaspoons cream tartar, or 3 spoons of baking powder. Bake on tins, an inch thick, and when taken from the oven, sprinkle with white sugar while hot.

Parker House Rolls.
Mrs. J. C. H., Chicago.

One pint scalded milk. Let it cool and add 2 tablespoons sugar, 2 of lard, 2 of yeast, a little salt. In winter mix in batter overnight; in morning knead; set to rise again, and at noon roll out very thin; cut in large rounds; put on a piece of butter, and lay the dough over. Let it rise again, and bake for tea. In summer mix early in the morning, instead of at night.

Rolls.
Aunt Lucy, Chicago.

Two quarts sifted flour; a little more than a pint milk; 1 tablespoon of lard; a little salt; a tablespoonful of white sugar, and ½ cup of yeast. Scald the milk; let stand to cool; put the sugar into the milk; rub the lard into the flour; make a hole in the center of the flour; pour in the milk and yeast; add the salt; sprinkle a little flour over the hole; set to rise; when very light mix in the rest of the flour; let rise again; about an hour before tea roll out very lightly; cut with the cover of a large baking-powder box; fold even (like a turn-over); let rise till very light, and bake in a quick oven 20 minutes.

French Rolls.
May Barnes, Cedar Rapids.

Into 1 pound of flour rub 2 ounces of butter and the whites of 3 eggs, well beaten; add a tablespoonful of good yeast, a little salt, and milk enough to make a stiff dough; cover and set it in a warm place till light, which will be an hour or more, according to the strength of the yeast. Cut into rolls, dip the edges into melted butter to keep them from sticking together, and bake in a quick oven.

Cinnamon Rolls.
Ethel, Iowa.

Take a piece of pie crust; roll it out; cut it in narrow strips; sprinkle cinnamon over it; roll it up tight; put it in a clean tin pan, which has been well oiled with butter; brown nicely, and bake. Then serve on the table.

Breakfast Rolls.
Stella, Beloit, Wis.

Flour, 2 quarts; sugar, 1 tablespoonful; butter, 1 tablespoonful; ½ cup of yeast; 1 pint scalded milk, or water, if milk is scarce, and a little salt. Set to rise until light; then knead until hard, and set to rise, and when wanted, make in rolls. Place a piece of butter between the folds, and bake in a slow oven.

Graham Breakfast Rolls.
Jeanette, Danville, Ills.

Two pounds potatoes, boiled and pressed, through a colander; 1 pint of water; ½ a cup of sugar; ½ a teaspoonful of salt; ½ a cup of yeast. Mix into a stiff dough, with Graham flour, and let rise over night. In the morning mold into small cakes, and when light bake.

Brown Bread.
Mrs. E. K., Blue Island avenue.

Three handfuls of corn-meal; 2 of flour or Graham; ½ cup sour milk; ½ cup molasses; ½ teaspoonful soda. Steam 2 hours. To be eaten warm, but is good cold.

J. A. S., Menasha, Wis.

Three cups of sweet milk, 1 cup of sour milk, 2 cups of Indian meal, 2 cups of rye-meal, ½ cup of good molasses, 1 teaspoon of soda or saleratus. Boil 3 hours hard in a pail or a tin pudding-dish.

Mrs. H. A. H., Chicago.

Three cups of sweet milk, 2 cups of corn meal, 2 cups of flour, 1 egg, ½ cup of molasses, 1 teaspoonful of salt, and 1 measure of Horsford's baking powder. Steam 3 hours; bake ½ an hour; let it stand ½ an hour before eating.

Boston Brown Bread.
Mrs. H. V. R., Chicago.

One quart of rye-meal (not flour), 2 quarts of corn-meal, ¾ of a cup of molasses, into which beat a teaspoonful of soda, add a teaspoonful of salt, and mix quite soft with boiling water, and bake.

Lou, Chicago.

Two cups of Indian meal, 3 of Graham flour, 1 tablespoonful soda, ½ cup Orleans molasses, a little salt; sour milk enough to make a stiff batter; steam 3½ hours in a pudding bucket; then put in oven to brown.

Corn Cake.
F. C., Chicago.

Two cups sour milk, 2 tablespoonfuls of molasses or brown sugar, 1 egg, 1 teaspoonful of saleratus, salt, ½ teaspoonful of ginger, 1½ cups of corn-meal, and 1½ cups of sifted flour. Bake in quick oven.

With fruit.—Pour 1 quart boiling water on 1 quart corn-meal, and stir quickly; salt to taste. Wet the hands, and form the dough into small round cakes ½ an inch thick. Bake in a hot oven. The addition of a few raspberries, or any sub-acid fruit, is a decided improvement. Sweet apples, chopped fine, are also excellent.

Rye Tea Cakes.
Mrs. B. H., Galva, Ill.

One pint sweet milk, 2 eggs well beaten, 1 tablespoonful of brown sugar, ½ a teaspoonful of salt; stir into this sufficient rye flour to make it as stiff as common griddle-cake batter. Bake in gem pans ½ an hour. Serve hot.

Graham Puffs.
Inkstand, Chicago.

One egg, 1 pint sweet milk, 1 pint Graham flour and a pinch of salt; beat the egg thoroughly; add the milk, then the flour gradually; beat the whole mixture briskly with an egg beater · pour into cast-iron gem pans, well greased and piping hot; bake in very hot oven. This mixture is just sufficient for 12 gems.

Oat Meal Cakes.
Mrs. M., Coldwater, Mich.

One cup rather fine oat-meal; 3 cups water, stirred together, and allowed to swell. Butter a pie-tin, and turn the batter in, and bake a ½ hour, or until a rich brown. Salt, of course.

Graham Cakes.
Mrs. Emily, Eau Claire, Wis.

Two cups sweet milk, 1 cup sweet cream, the white of 1 egg beaten to froth, ½ a spoonful of salt, dessertspoonful baking powder; stir in sifted Graham flour until quite thick; bake in muffin-rings or gem-tins until well browned on top.

Oat Meal Gems.
Souella M., Eagle, Wis.

Take 1 cup of oat-meal and soak it over night in 1 cup of water; in the morning add 1 cup of sour milk, 1 teaspoon of saleratus, 1 cup of flour, a little salt. They are baked in irons as other gems and muffins. If on first trial you find them moist and sticky, add a little more flour, as some flour thickens more than others.

Graham Gems.
Mrs. M., Coldwater, Mich.

Take 3 teacups of soft water or boiled well water, and 4½ teacups best Graham flour; beat together about 10 minutes. Have cast-iron gem pans on the stove sissing hot; put in each pan a tiny piece of butter, and fill even full with the batter; have the oven very hot when you put them in, and then gradually allow the heat to decrease. This makes the pans twice full; bake 20 minutes. We have to vary the flour a little at every fresh bagful, or it does not swell alike.

Aunt Emma, Chicago.

To 1 quart of Graham flour add ½ pint fine white flour, and enough milk or water, a little warm, to make a thick batter; no salt or baking powder. Have your oven hotter than for biscuit, and your gem-pans standing in the oven till you get ready. Beat batter thoroughly, grease your pans, and drop in while the irons are smoking hot. Bake quickly a nice brown.

Graham or Rye Gems.
Mrs. R. J. G., Onslow, Iowa.

One egg, 1 pint sour milk, with a few spoonfuls cream added, 1 teaspoonful soda, a little salt, and enough Graham or rye meal to make a stiff batter: bake in gem-pans in a quick oven.

Graham Cookies.
Mrs. R. J. G., Onslow, Iowa.

Two cups sugar, 1 cup sour cream, ½ teaspoonful

soda; mix quickly, roll and bake. These require less heat and more time in baking than when white flour is used.

Graham Crackers.
Mrs. R. J. G., Onslow, Iowa.

Seven cups Graham, 1 cup thick sweet cream (or butter), 1 pint sweet milk, 2 teaspoonfuls baking powder. Rub the baking powder into the flour. Add the cream with a little salt, then the milk; mix well, and roll as thin as soda-crackers; cut in any shape; bake quickly; then leave about the stove for a few hours to dry thoroughly.

Rich Waffles.
Mary, Lee Center, Ill.

Make a thin paste with 8 ounces of flour, 6 ounces of pulverized sugar, 2 eggs, a few drops of essence to flavor, ½ a liquor-glass of brandy or rum, and milk. Warm and butter both sides of the mold, put some of the paste into it; close it gently, set it on the fire, turn it over to heat both sides equally, dust them with sugar when done, and serve either warm or cold. It takes hardly a minute for each with a good fire.

Rye Drops Fried.
Julia Rive, Tolono.

One cup sour milk or buttermilk, 3 tablespoonfuls sugar, 1 of butter if buttermilk is not used, 1 egg, scant teaspoonful soda, and one of cinnamon; add rye flour sufficient to make a stiff batter. Take it up by the tablespoonful and drop into boiling hot lard, first dipping the spoon into the hot lard to prevent the dough sticking to the spoon.

Graham or Rye Mush.
Mrs. R. J. G., Onslow, Iowa.

Stir Graham or rye meal into boiling water, with a little salt, till quite thick: cook a few minutes. This is very nice either with poached eggs or butter and sugar.

Oatmeal Mush.
Mrs. R. J. G., Onslow, Iowa.

Soak the oatmeal over night in enough water to wet it, in the morning stir into boiling water. Cook a few minutes.

Mrs. S. M. B., Chicago.

Three cups of meal will make a generous dish for a party of 4 or 5 persons. When it has cooked about 2 hours in a double boiler, salt it thoroughly, and at the end of three hours it should be found very stiff and dry as possible, turned out to cool and mold; cut in slices thin as can be handled without breaking, fry in butter and lard, equal parts, or ⅜ butter. The rich brown of these crisp bits will prove tempting to the veriest epicure.

Whole Wheat.
Mrs. Louise, Chicago.

Either boil it slowly until quite soft, or bake 6 or 8 hours, the same as beans, omitting the pork; or as a pudding, with milk sufficient to allow it to swell, or about 2 quarts of milk to a pint of wheat. Sweeten to taste, and add a few drops of vanilla or lemon flavoring, if desired.

Corn Bread.
Mima C. Morer, Cleveland.

Two cups sour milk; ¾ of a cup molasses; 2 cups of corn meal; 1½ cups of white flour; small tablespoon of soda, dissolved in sour milk. Salt. Steam 3 hours. To be eaten hot. Slice and steam when you wish to warm it up.

Mrs. A. P. F., Highland Park, Ills.

Two cups meal, 1 cup flour, ¼ cup sugar, 3 teaspoons baking-powder, a little salt, moisten with sweet milk until like cup-cake. Bake in a quick oven, or it will not be nice.

Rye Bread.
Mrs. C. G. S., Rock River Falls, Ills.

First scald 2 coffee-cups of corn meal with boiling water to a thick batter. When this is cool, add ¼ of a bowl of light sponge—taken from bread-sponge prepared with potatoes that has raised over night—½ teacup of sugar, 3 teaspoons of soda and salt. This stir as stiff with rye flour as can be stirred with a spoon. Let this raise very light, and then add as much rye again as can be worked in with the hands without kneading. Drop in a buttered pan, and bake slowly for 1½ hours.

Graham Bread.
Blanche, Chicago.

One pint yeast, same as used for white bread; stir in a pint of warm water and a little salt, then add Graham flour until you have a thick batter. Bake 15 minutes longer than the same size loaf of white bread. It will not rise as much as other bread.

Mrs R. J. G., Onslow, Iowa.

Graham 3 quarts, 2 quarts warm water, ½ pint yeast, 1 teaspoonful soda, ½ pint sugar. Mix with a spoon. Pour into deep tins, well greased, and set in a warm place till quite light. Bake with a steady, moderate heat two hours. This recipe makes 3 good loaves.

Mrs. E. E., Wisconsin.

Take the "sponge" of white bread when light, enough for 1 loaf or 2, as you wish, and mix in enough Graham flour to make a moderately stiff loaf; place in a pan, and, when light, bake. You can add a little sugar or molasses if you like. Can also make very nice rye bread in the same way.

Bread for Dyspeptics.
C. M. W., Hudson, Mich.

For 1 loaf, 1 pint of attrition flour; 1 pint wheat flour; prepare with Horsford's Bread Preparation according to directions which come with it. adding salt, mixing soft, with sweet milk, with the hands, and bake quickly. To be used when a day old.

Oatmeal Gruel.
Mrs. W. B. B., Kalamazoo, Mich.

Take 2 ounces of oatmeal and 1½ pints of water. Rub the meal in a basin with the back of a spoon, in a small quantity of water, pouring off the fluid after the coarser particles are settled, but while the milkiness continues, repeat the operation until the milkiness disappears. Next put the washings into a pan, stir until they boil, and a soft, thick mucilage is formed. Sweeten to taste.

Milk Sponge Bread.
Adelaide, Negaunee.

Put a pint of boiling water in a pitcher, with a teaspoonful of sugar, ¼ teaspoonful salt, and the same of soda; let it stand till you can bear your finger in it; then add flour to make a thick batter; beat it hard for 2 minutes. Now place the pitcher in a kettle of hot water—not hot enough to scald the mixture; keep the water at the same temperature till the emptyings are light. If set early in the morning they will be ready, if watched carefully, at 11 o'clock to make a sponge, the same as for other bread, with a quart of very warm milk. Let this sponge get very light; then make into loaves and set to rise again, taking care they do not get too light this time before putting in the oven, or the bread will be dry and tasteless.

Yeast Bread.
R. C. F., Chicago.

At about 4 o'clock in the afternoon take 3 quarts of good flour and 1½ quarts lukewarm water—or milk will make whiter bread—and a little salt. Place a cake of strictly fresh yeast in a small dish of the water. Stir your flour and water into a thick batter, mixing in the yeast as soon as it is soft, leaving dry flour around the edge to keep it warm. Then cover and set away in a warm place in the summer, or by the stove in the winter, until it begins to rise nicely—say 9 or 10 o'clock in the evening. Then mix thick, and knead about half as much as to bake. Then cover and set away again until morning. By 6 o'clock you will find your dish more than full, unless it is large. Then knead well and put in baking-tins, and set by the stove to rise. When light enough put in the oven and keep it evenly heated until done. This will make 3 good loaves.

Salt-Rising Bread.
C. M. W., Hudson, Mich.

Take newly-ground middlings, put 6 heaping teaspoonfuls of it in a coffee-cup; add 1 teaspoon of sugar; 1 saltspoon of salt; ¼ saltspoon of soda, mix thoroughly; pour boiling water in the mixture, stirring it well together until it will nearly fill the cup; remove the spoon; cover the cup of dough; set it where it will keep warm, not scald. Set it Friday morning, and it will be light for Saturday's baking. If in a hurry, set in a dish of warm water. Now put in bread-pan flour

COOKERY—BREAD.

enough for bread; add salt; take 1 quart of boiling water for three loaves, and turn into the middle of your flour, stirring in slowly; put enough cold water (or milk) to cool sufficiently to bear your finger in it; then add middlings—stir in well; cover with some of the flour, and set in a warm place. When light enough, mix soft into loaves; grease bread-pans; also top of the loaves, which makes a tender upper crust; cut gashes quite deep across the loaves, and it will rise evenly; set near the stove, and when light enough, bake ¾ of an hour.

R. C. F., Chicago.

Take ½ teaspoonful salt, 1 tablespoonful sugar, 1 pint lukewarm water, and flour enough to make a good batter. Cover closely and set the receptacle in a jar of warm water and cover that also. Let it remain until it rises, then use as any other rising. Flour mixed up with milk will make whiter bread than when mixed with water.

Housekeeper 40 years, Virginia, Ills.

In early morning take a teacupful of new milk; pour boiling water in until it is blood warm; put in a small quarter teaspoon of salt; the same of sugar; then stir in 1 large tablespoonful of Graham flour, or corn-meal, and 2 tablespoonfuls of fine flour, or until it is as thick as pancake batter; mix it all in a quart cup, and set it to rise. Keep it of an equal heat by setting the cup in warm water; if water gathers on top dust a little flour and stir; it will rise by noon. Mix as other bread; mold and put in pans at once; let stand until light, when it is ready for the oven. If you have no milk, water will do for the rising.

Betsy, Inavale, Neb.

The recipe: In the morning take a quart dish and scald it out; then put in a pint of warm water; put in a teaspoonful of salt; stir flour enough in to make a thick batter; set the dish in a kettle of warm water, and where it will keep of the same temperature—just warm enough to bear your hand in. If the flour is good it will be at the top of the dish in 2 hours; then take flour enough in a pan to make 3 loaves of bread;

make a hole in the middle; put in the yeast, and the same dish full of warm water; stir it up thick with a spoon, and cover it with some of the flour, and set it to rise. When light, mold it into loaves, and set in a warm place to rise again. When light enough, bake ¾ of an hour.

CAKES, COOKIES, ETC.

Doughnuts.
Cousin Nell, Chicago.

SIX cups of flour; 1½ cups of sugar; 3 teaspoons of baking powder; 1 teaspoon of salt; butter the size of ½ an egg; mix thoroughly; then add 4 eggs well beaten, and moisten with sweet milk until a soft dough. Flavor with nutmeg or cinnamon.

Aunt Nellie Bly, St. Joseph, Mich.

Break 2 eggs in a bowl, with 1 large cup of sugar, 1 cup sour milk, 1 teaspoon soda, spices to suit the taste. Mix *very* soft. That is the secret of good fried cakes. Have your fat hot; drop in 5 or 6; they will almost turn over themselves they are so light; keep some going in and some coming out all the time; the last ones cool the fat, so the first ones do not get so brown; but cook through.

Mrs. W., Green Bay.

I set my sponge for them about 2 or 3 o'clock, so I can fry them the next forenoon. Make a sponge, using 1 quart water and 1 cake yeast. Let it rise until very light (about 5 hours is usually sufficient). Then add 1 coffee-cup full of lard, 2 of white sugar, 3 large mashed potatoes or 2 eggs (the potatoes are nicer), and a small nutmeg. Let rise again until *very* light. Roll and cut, or pull off bits of dough and shape as you like. Lay enough to fry at one time on a floured plate, and set in the oven to warm. Drop in boiling lard, and fry longer than cakes made with baking powder. If the dough is light enough, and you heat it before

COOKERY—CAKES, COOKIES, ETC.

dropping in the lard, I am sure your doughnuts will be delicious.

Mrs. N. N., Chicago.

Mix your dough with sour milk and saleratus, as for biscuits, with a small quantity of sugar and spice; fry in lard, of course; if you are dyspeptic omit the sugar.

Mrs. Emily, Eau Claire, Wis.

Three eggs, 1 cup sugar, 1 pint of new milk, salt, nutmeg, and flour enough to permit the spoon to stand upright in the mixture; add 2 teaspoonfuls baking powder and beat until very light. Drop by the dessertspoonful into boiling lard. These will not absorb a bit of fat, and are the least pernicious of the doughnut family.

Mrs. N. W. H., Chicago.

One cup sugar, 1 cup sweet milk, 1 egg, 1 teaspoonful soda dissolved in a little of the milk, 3 tablespoonfuls of melted lard; add a little salt and nutmeg, and flour enough to roll well. Have ready a kettle of *boiling* lard in which to fry them.

Mrs. L. J. C., Chicago.

Whole wheat flour: One heaping teacupful sugar; 3 tablespoonfuls melted shortening (½ butter and ½ lard), 2 eggs, 1 quart of cold-ground whole-wheat flour, a little nutmeg, 1 cup sweet milk with a small teaspoonful of soda dissolved in it, 2 spoonfuls of cream tartar mixed and sifted with the flour. Fry in part suet and part lard.

Cookies.
J. A. S., Menasha, Wis.

Two cups of white sugar, 1 cup of butter, 1 cup of sweet milk, 2 spoons of baking powder, nutmeg; flour enough to roll out; better if rolled out thin, and a hot oven to bake in.

Busy Bee, Ottumwa, Iowa.

Two teacups sugar, 1 of butter, 1 of sour milk, and soda to sweeten it, ½ nutmeg; roll thin; cut with cutter with ring in center; bake a pretty brown.

Fanchon, LaFayette, Ind.

Two cups of sugar, 1 cup of butter, 3 eggs, not quite a teaspoonful of soda, dissolved into 2 tablespoonfuls of water; nutmeg to taste, and flour enough to roll out soft. Cut into cakes, and bake in a moderately hot oven.

Mrs. Emily, Eau Claire, Wis.

Whites of 2 eggs, 1 large cup of milk, 1 cup of sugar. ½ cup of butter, 2 teaspoonful baking powder, flavor with vanilla, rose or nutmeg; flour enough for thick batter; beat thoroughly; drop in buttered pans; dust granulated sugar on top, and bake with dispatch.

C. M. W., Hudson, Mich.

Ginger Cookies of Attrition Flour—1 cup New Orleans molasses; ½ cup sugar; ½ cup butter; ½ cup water; 1 egg; 1 heaping teaspoon of soda, stirred into the molasses; and 1 heaping teaspoon of ginger. Mix till smooth; roll thin, and bake quick.

Mrs. W. S. G., Baraboo, Wis.

One cup butter; 2 cups sugar; 4 eggs; 4 cups flour; 3 tablespoons milk; 3 teaspoons baking-powder. Rub the flour and butter thoroughly together; cream the butter and sugar; beat the eggs separately; add to the above, with a little nutmeg and cinnamon, or any seasoning preferred. Sift in the flour and baking-powder, and add enough flour to mold and roll out. These cookies will keep fresh 2 weeks, and if the milk is left out a month.

Mrs. M., Mendota, Ills.

One cup butter and 4 of flour; rub well together; add 1 teaspoon of soda; beat together ½ cup sugar and 2 eggs; mix all together; roll thin and bake.

A plainer kind: 1 egg, 1 cup sugar, ½ cup butter, ½ cup sweet milk, ½ teaspoon soda, 1 teaspoon cream tartar; flour to mix soft.

Mrs. E. K., Blue Island.

One cup sugar; ½ cup lard or butter; ½ cup sour milk; ½ teaspoonful soda; just flour enough to roll, baking quickly. Add any flavoring you wish. No eggs are required, so don't imagine I left them out. These are very nice if grated or prepared cocoanut is added.

Georgia H., Chicago.

One cup sour cream; 1 cup butter; 2 cups sugar; 2 eggs; 1 teaspoon soda; flour, and flavoring to suit.

Mrs. C. E., Minonk.

Cream 1½ cups; 2 cups sugar; 2 eggs; ½ teaspoonful soda. Knead soft. They will keep moist.

Gingersnaps.
L. B. C., Fon du Lac, Wis.

One coffee-cup New Orleans molasses; 1 cup butter; 1 cup sugar; place them on the stove, and let it come to a boil. Then take off immediately, and add teaspoon of soda, and a tablespoon of ginger. Roll thin and bake quickly.

Georgia H., Chicago.

One cup molasses; 1 cup brown sugar; 1 cup melted lard; 2 large spoons of ginger; 2 spoons of alum, dissolved in hot water; 1 teaspoon salt; 5 teaspoons soda; mix with flour into a stiff paste.

Mrs. C. E., Minonk, Ills.

Two cups molasses; 1 of butter; 1 teaspoon ginger; ½ teaspoonful soda. Put all into a pan, and set on the stove until it boils up; then take off, and put in the soda. Roll thin; bake quickly.

Mrs. W. S. G., Baraboo, Wis.

One cup molasses, 1 cup brown sugar; ½ cup lard and butter melted together, 3 tablespoonfuls ginger, 1 teaspoonful cinnamon; ½ teaspoonful cloves; 1 teaspoon soda dissolved in ½ a cup of boiling water; thicken with flour; roll and bake.

Aunt Betsy, Chicago.

Take 1 pint of New Orleans molasses; 2 tablespoons of lard, and 1 tablespoon of ginger; let it come to a boil, and when cool add one teaspoon of soda (dissolved in a little water) and flour enough to make a soft dough; roll thin and bake in a quick oven.

Leona, Canton, Ills.

1 pint of New Orleans molasses; 1 cup of butter; 1

teaspoon soda; one or more spoons of ginger. Let them boil up together, and when cool add flour to roll.

Soft Ginger Cookies.
Jennie, Chicago.

Two teacups New Orleans molasses; 1 teacup of melted lard; 1 teacup of boiling water; 4 teaspoonfuls of soda bought in bulk; 1 teaspoonful of ginger. Pour the boiling water on the soda; do not knead too stiff. Bake with steady heat.

Cheap Ginger Cookies.
Mary Jones, Delavan.

One cup molasses, 1 cup brown sugar, 1 cup warm water, 1 cup lard, 2 tablespoons ginger, 1 tablespoon soda (dissolved in water), 1 teaspoon powdered alum, put in last. Mix soft. Bake quickly.

Ginger Bread.
Jennie, Chicago.

Two teacups New Orleans molasses; 2 cups boiling water; ¾ cup of melted butter; 1 tablespoonful of ginger; two teaspoonfuls of soda. Add flour enough to make a smooth batter. Beat well.

Mrs. M., Mendota.

Butter, 1½ cups (or lard), 1 cup boiling water poured over it, 2 cups baking molasses, 2 teaspoons soda, 2 teaspoons ginger; flour to make about like cake-batter. Spread molasses over the top while hot, after it is baked. This is not rich, but very good if eaten fresh. It is not so good when old.

H. V. R., Chicago.

One egg well beaten, 1 cup molasses, 1 cup sugar, 1 cup of butter, 1 cup of cold tea, 2 even teaspoons of soda, flour enough to mix about the consistency of cake.

Better baked in 2 sheets than 1, as when too thick the outside will be burned or too hard, before it is done through.

P. P. C., Chicago.

One teacup sugar; 1 cup butter; 1 cup molasses; 3 eggs (yolks and whites beaten separately until very light); 1 cup sweet milk; 4 teacups flour; 3 teaspoons baking-powder; 1 tablespoon ginger; 1 grated nutmeg. Bake in a rather large bread-pan, in a moderate oven.

J. S., Chicago.

New Orleans molasses 1½ cups; brown sugar ½ cup; ¼ cup butter; 1 egg well beaten; 1 tablespoon of soda, dissolved in a cup of boiling water; nearly a tablespoon each of ginger and cinnamon; mix like cake and bake in a moderately hot oven.

Mary, Chicago.

Melt ½ a cup of butter in 1 cup of molasses and 1 of sugar, allowing the mixture to become hot; then add 1 tablespoon of ground ginger, one teaspoon of ground cinnamon, 1 cup of sweet milk, 5 cups of flour stirred in with a full ½ teaspoon of soda. Bake in two flat tin pans, or gem-irons. Teacup I measure with holds ½ a pint.

Coffee Cakes.
Garnet, Delavan, Wis.

Three eggs, well beaten; 2 cups brown sugar; 1 cup butter; 1 cup of milk; 1 teaspoonful of soda; 2 teaspoons of cream-of-tartar. Work this to a stiff dough, and roll out to about a ¼ inch in thickness. Sift ground cinnamon over evenly; then roll up like roll jelly cake. Cut slices about a ¼ inch thick from the roll; drop into granulated sugar, and bake thoroughly with sugared side up.

Mrs. J. C. H., Chicago.

Coffee 1½ cups, usual strength; 1½ cups sugar; ½ cup molasses; 1 cup of chopped raisins; one of currants; *nearly* 1 cup butter; 1 teaspoon soda; 1 nutmeg; a little citron, cinnamon, cloves, spices of any kind you have. First stir together sugar, molasses, spices, fruit and butter, and pour on the coffee hot. Add flour to make stiff as fruit cake. It improves with age.

Breakfast Coffee Cakes.
Dickie, Aurora.

Three cups bread sponge; ½ cup butter; little sugar; egg. Roll thin as baking-powder biscuit. Cut out with tumbler or cake-cutter; sprinkle over a little sugar, cinnamon, and little bits of butter. As our family is small, I only use ½ the recipe.

Jumbles.
Agnes, Chicago.

One and a half cups sugar, ½ a cup butter, 2 eggs, ½ teaspoon soda, 1 of cream-of-tartar (dissolved in a little sweet milk), flour enough to make like pie-crust. Bake in waffle-irons. Fill the little holes with light and dark jelly, alternately.

Jennie R., Marion.

Two cups of sugar, 1 of butter, 1 of milk, 4 eggs. 1 teaspoonful of baking-powder, flour to make it stiff enough to roll out, cut into shape and bake in a quick oven.

Crullers.
Mrs. E. K., Blue Island.

Three eggs; 1 cup sugar; 4 tablespoonfuls melted lard, 6 sweet milk, 2 tablespoonfuls baking powder; any flavoring you wish, and flour to roll nicely. I beat the eggs and sugar together first; then add the lard, beating well; then the milk; put my baking-powder in the flour, and sift it in, stirring it with a spoon as long as I can, as I dislike using my hands.

Three fourths of a pound granulated sugar, ¼ pound butter, 1 cupful milk, 5 eggs, pinch of salt, teaspoonful vanilla extract, nutmeg to taste, 3 pounds sifted flour; mix butter, sugar, and part of the milk to a very creamy batter; then the eggs, rest of milk and flavoring, then some of the flour, and beat till very light, adding the flour till very stiff; then with the hands knead in nearly all the flour, reserving a little for flouring the pastry board; cut off a lump, roll out ½ inch thick, and cut in pieces 3 inches long and 2 wide, twist in fancy shapes, drop few at a time in boiling hot lard, sift powdered sugar over them, when cool slip on a large meat-dish, and carefully, as they are crisp and break easily. This quantity requires nearly 4 pounds of lard to cook them; keep the fat boiling; slices of peeled white potato dropped in the fat absorbs the sediment from the dough that darkens the fat; take the potato out when black and put in another piece.

Indian Meal Crullers.

One and a half teacupfuls boiling milk poured over 2 teacupfuls Indian-meal; when it cools add 2 cupfuls wheat flour, 1 of butter, 1½ of sugar, 3 eggs, and a tablespoonful nutmeg or cinnamon, if not stiff enough, add equal portions of wheat and meal; let it rise till very light; roll it about ¼ an inch thick; cut it into small diamond-shaped cakes, and boil them in hot lard.

Pumpkin Loaf.
C. M. W., Hudson, Mich.

For 2 loaves, take 2 cups buttermilk; 3 cups each of wheat flour and corn meal, 1 cup stewed pumpkin, 1 cup molasses, ½ cup butter, 2 eggs, 1 tablespoon soda. Steam 1½ hours, then bake ½ hour.

Strawberry Short Cake.
Theo. C. C., Chicago.

First prepare the berries by picking; after they have been well washed—the best way to wash them is to hold the boxes under the faucet and let a gentle stream of water run over them into an earthen bowl—then drain, and pick them into an earthen bowl; now take the potato-masher and bruise them and cover with a thick layer of white sugar; now set them aside till the cake is made. Take a quart of sifted flour; ½ a cup of sweet butter; 1 egg, well beaten; 3 teaspoonfuls of baking-powder, and milk enough to make a rather stiff dough; knead well, and roll with the rolling-pin till about 1 inch thick; bake till a nice brown, and when done, remove it to the table; turn it out of the pan; with a light, sharp knife, cut it down lengthwise and crossways; now run the knife through it, and lay it open for a few moments, just to let the steam escape (the steam ruins the color of the berries); then set the bottom crust on the platter; cover thickly with the berries, an inch and a half deep; lay the top crust on the fruit; dust thickly with powdered sugar, and if any berry juice is left in the bowl, pour it round the cake, not over it, and you will have a delicious short cake.

Scotch Short Cake.
Mrs. W. B. Fyfe, Pontiac, Ill.

Take ½ a pound of slightly salted butter, and 1 pound of flour; then mix flour and butter with hands; then add 4 ounces of loaf sugar, and work all into a smooth ball; then roll out, until it is an inch thick; prick over with a fork, and pinch round the edges, and bake for ½ an hour in oven, with a moderate fire, in a round or square pan, according to taste.

Sponge Cake.
Mrs. Angie Mackey, Rome, N. Y.

Two eggs thoroughly beaten with 1 cup of sugar, ½ cup of boiling water, sift 2 teaspoonfuls baking powder through an even teacup sifted flour, season with lemon or vanilla, 1 more egg for layer cake, used as follows: Save two whites for frosting, using the 2 yolks and another egg for the cake part. Bake in jelly-cake tins; whip the whites up, stir in sugar, not enough to make hard frosting.

If you wish cocoanut cake, spread the frosting on each layer and sprinkle over the cocoanut. On the top layer of frosting sprinkle the cocoanut thick.

If you desire chocolate cake grate a ½ teacupful and stir in with the frosting; then spread between the layers of cake and on top. Be careful not to get too much water, and to bake in a quick oven.

Edna, Chicago.

Twelve eggs; the weight of 10 eggs in powdered sugar; the weight of 6 eggs in sifted flour; the grated rind and juice of 1 lemon; beat the yolk of eggs and sugar together to a light froth. This is essential. Add the whites of the eggs, well beaten, then the lemon, and a pinch of salt; stir in the flour gradually until well mixed; bake in long, narrow pans three inches deep, on buttered paper; fill the pans; ⅔ bake in a quick oven. The shape and depth of the pans have a great deal to do with the quality of the cake.

C. M. W., Hudson, Mich.

Take 3 eggs; beat 3 minutes; then add 1½ cups sugar, and beat 5 minutes; add 1 teacup flour, and 1 teaspoon cream tartar, and beat 3 minutes; add ½ teaspoon soda, dissolved in ½ cup cold water, and another cup of flour; beat enough to mix well. Flavor and bake in a deep pan in a quick oven.

Mrs. S. E., Chicago.

One cup of sugar and 5 eggs, beaten together ½ an

hour; add 1 cup of flour and a little salt; beat well and bake immediately.

A Farmer's Wife, Mendota.

Three eggs, 1 cup of sugar, even off 1 tablespoonful of cold water, 1 heaping cup of flour, 1 teaspoonful of baking-powder. Bake 15 or 20 minutes—not longer.

Corn Starch Cake.
Daily Reader, Hillsdale, Mich.

Four eggs—whites only; 1 cup of powdered sugar; ½ cup of butter; ¾ cup corn-starch; ½ cup sweet milk; 1 cup flour; 2 teaspoonfuls baking powder, lemon or rosewater flavoring. Cream the butter and sugar thoroughly either with the hand or a silver spoon; mix the corn-starch with the milk, and add. Then add the eggs, beaten stiff; next the sifted flour, into which the baking-powder has been stirred. Mix all well; bake nicely, and call in your friends to help eat it, as this, like all corn-starch cake, is not fit to eat after the second day, and is much the best the same day it is baked.

Cream Puffs.
Mrs. Eve, Kalamazoo, Mich.

One-half pint cold water, in which rub smooth 6 ounces of flour; put it into a spider with 4 ounces of butter, and stir it continually over a fire not too hot, till it is thoroughly cooked. It will resemble a lump of putty and cleave off the spider like a pancake. Cool this lump, and add 4 eggs. Beat well, and then drop on a buttered tin in neat, compact little "dabs," far enough apart not to touch when they rise. Have the oven about as hot as for cookies, and in turning them lift up the tin. If you shove them before they are set you will have pancakes. They should be hollow balls. Bake them long enough so they will not fall when removed, and cool them on brown paper as quickly as possible, so they won't sweat. To fill them take ½ pint milk; 2 beaten eggs; ¼ cup of flour or corn-starch wet smoothly; 1 cup sugar; lemon or vanilla flavor; cook it in a tin pail in a kettle of hot water, and stir it so it will be smooth. When both are cold, open the puff with a sharp knife; just a little slit on the side, and fill in one tablespoonful of custard.

Almond Drops.
German, Chicago.

Take 9 ounces of flour; six ounces of sugar; ½ pound of butter; four eggs; 2 teaspoonfuls of baking-powder. Stir butter and sugar first; rub the powder into the flour, and add the rest. Pour into square tin pans, filling them about ½ an inch, and strew cinnamon, sugar, and sliced almonds over it. The almonds must be previously scalded. Bake a light brown, and, when done, cut into squares.

Anise Drops.
German, Chicago.

Two cupfuls of granulated sugar; 3 eggs; 3 cupfuls of flour, and 1 teaspoon of anise-seed. Beat sugar and eggs well for ½ an hour; then add the other ingredients; drop on buttered pans, and bake in a moderate oven. The secret here lies in beating rapidly and thoroughly. These will make small cakes, and each teaspoonful is to be dropped separately.

Lady Fingers.
Mrs. Sarah B., Chicago.

Four ounces of sugar; 4 yolks of eggs, mix well; 3 ounces of flour; a little salt. Beat the 4 whites to a stiff froth, stir the whites into the mixture a little at a time until all is in. Butter a shallow pan. Squirt through a confectioner's syringe or a little piece of paper rolled up. Dust with sugar, and bake in a not too hot oven.

Indian Meal Pound Cake.
Fannie Sands, Wis.

Sift 1 pint of yellow corn-meal and ½ pint wheat flour, into which first put teaspoonful baking powder, and a small spoonful salt; 1 grated nutmeg; 1 tablespoonful ground cinnamon; put ¾ of a pound granulated sugar and ½ a pound butter together. Beat 8 eggs very light, and add to the butter and sugar, alternately, with the meal—little at a time—and a ½ cup milk, and have dish or pan well buttered; bake in a moderate oven. Takes a long time to bake.

Bread Cake.
Lizzie Bacon, Iowa.

Four cups dough, 2 cups sugar, 1 cup butter, 1 cup cream, 2 eggs, 1 teaspoon saleratus. Mix with the hands, and add a little flour, also fruit and spices to suit the taste, and let it rise well before baking.

Lincoln Cake.
Fannie T., Springfield, Ill.

Rub 1 pound sugar and ¾ pound butter together; add the yolk 6 well-beaten eggs, 2 cupfuls sour cream, with 1 teaspoonful soda dissolved in a little boiling water and stirred into it just before adding to the cake; 1 teaspoonful each of nutmeg and cinnamon, and 1 pound sifted flour; 1 tablespoonful rose water; ½ a pound citron cut and dredged with flour, and lastly, the whites of the eggs, which must be beaten very stiff before being added; then beat all thoroughly and bake in square shallow pans.

White and Yellow Mountain Cake.
Marion, Davenport, Iowa.

Two cups sugar, ⅔ cup butter, whites of 7 eggs, well beaten, ¾ cup sweet milk, 2 cups flour, 1 cup cornstarch, 2 teaspoons baking powder. Bake in jelly cake tins. Frosting: Whites of 3 eggs and some sugar, beaten together—not quite as stiff as for frosting; spread over the cake; add some grated cocoanut; then put your cakes together; put cocoanut or frosting for the top.

Yellow mountain: Yolks of 10 eggs, 1 cup butter, 2 of sugar, 1 of milk, 3 of flour, 1 teaspoon soda, 2 of cream tartar.

Jelly Cake.
Jessie, Joliet, Ill.

One cup milk, ½ cup chocolate, ½ cup sugar, yolk 1 egg, teaspoonful corn-starch. Mix well together, and boil until quite thick. When cold, put between the layers as for jelly cake, with the addition of a little butter. Water can be used instead of milk. Also by taking ¼ of the cake, putting chocolate in to make it a dark brown; this, with alternate layers of the remaining white, makes a very nice cake. Frosting can be made brown by adding chocolate, after the sugar has been mixed with the eggs.

Fruit Cake from Dough.
Mrs. R. L. B., Cedar Rapids, Iowa.

Two cups sugar, 1 cup butter, 1 pint of dough, 2 eggs, 1 teaspoon soda; as much fruit as you wish; spices to suit taste; use flour enough to make as stiff as common fruit cake; set in a warm place to raise for 1 hour. Bake in a moderate oven.

Marble Cake.
Mrs. R. L. B., Cedar Rapids, Iowa.

Light part: White sugar, 1½ cups; butter, ½ cup; sweet milk, ½ cup; soda, ½ teaspoon; cream of tartar, 1 teaspoon; whites of 4 eggs; flour, 2½ cups; beat the eggs and sugar together; mix the cream of tartar with the flour, and dissolve the soda in the milk. Dark part: Brown sugar, 1 cup; molasses, ½ cup; sour milk, ½ cup; soda, ½ teaspoon; flour, browned, 2½ cups; yolks of 4 eggs; cloves and cinnamon, ground, each ¼ teaspoon; ingredients mixed the same as light part. When both are prepared, put in the cake-pan alternate layers of each, or put them in spots on each other, making what is called leopard cake, until all is used, then bake as usual.

Fruit Cake Without Eggs.
Hattie, Aurora, Ill.

One cup of brown sugar, 1 of sour milk, 1 of raisins, 2 of flour, 4 tablespoons of melted butter, 1 teaspoon each of cinnamon, cloves, nutmeg and soda.

Molasses Fruit Cake.
Dew Rose, Chicago.

One cup molasses; 1¾ cups light brown sugar; 1 cup cold water. Boil the molasses, sugar and butter together, and set aside to cool; flour as thick as a pound-cake; then add eggs; beat this well; then add 1 pound raisins, 1 of currants, and ½ of citron, with 2 heaping teaspoons of flour mixed through the fruit; bake nearly 2 hours.

Fruit Cake.
Sky-Blue Cardinal, Chicago.

Put 1 teaspoon of soda in a coffee cup; add 5 tea-

COOKERY—CAKES, COOKIES, ETC.

spoons of hot water, 4 of melted butter, and fill with molasses. Make pretty stiff with flour; then stir in this all it will hold of chopped raisins, Zante currants, citron, and 1 teaspoon each of nutmeg, cinnamon, and a pinch of cloves. Bake from 3 to 4 hours in a very slow oven. (Put buttered paper in bottom of pan.) The longer this cake is kept the better it is.

Mrs. C. A. L., LaCrosse, Wis.

One pound each of sugar, butter and flour; 2 pounds of raisins and currants; 1 pound of citron; 9 eggs; ½ pint brandy; ½ an ounce each of nutmeg, cinnamon, ground cloves and mace; beat the eggs separate; stir the white and the flour in last.

Lou, Joliet, Ill.

Eight eggs beaten separate; 1 pound of butter; 2 pounds of sugar; 2 pounds of raisins; 1½ pounds of figs; 1 pound Zante currants; ½ pound citron; 1 pint of brandy; 1¾ pounds of flour; 2 teaspoonfuls of soda; nutmeg and cinnamon, each 1½ teaspoonfuls.

Farmers' Fruit Cake.
S., Aurora, Ill.

Soak 3 cups of dried apples over night; chop slightly in the morning; then simmer 2 hours in 2 cups of molasses; add 2 eggs, 1 cup sugar, 1 cup sweet milk, ¾ cup butter, 2 teaspoons soda, flour to make stiff batter; spice to suit the taste; bake in a moderate oven.

Black Cake.
Anna R., Pittsfield, Ill.

One pint molasses; 1 pint brown sugar; 1 pint of butter; 1 pint sour milk; 3 eggs; 2 teaspoons soda; cloves, nutmeg, cinnamon, raisins. Make it very stiff, and bake in a slow oven. This will make 2 large cakes.

Mary E., Mattoon, Ill.

One pound browned flour; 1 pound brown sugar; 1 pound citron; 2 pounds currants; 3 pounds stoned raisins; ¾ pound of butter; 1 teacup of molasses; 2 teaspoonfuls mace; 2 teaspoonfuls cinnamon; 1 teaspoonful cloves; 1 teaspoonful soda; 12 eggs. This is an excellent recipe, and will make 2 large loaves. It will keep a year (if locked up).

Delicate Cake.
Cousin Anna, Grand Rapids, Mich.

Whites of 4 eggs; 1 cup of milk—running over; ½ cup butter; 2 cups sugar; 2½ cups flour; heaping teaspoonful baking powder. This makes 2 loaves. If you want it *very* nice, use 1 cup of corn-starch in place of one of flour.

Caramel Cake.
Lillie W., Engelwood, Ill.

Three cups of sugar, 1½ cups of butter, 1 cup of milk, 4½ cups of flour, 5 eggs, two teaspoonfuls of baking-powder. Bake in layers.

Caramel for filling: 1½ cups brown sugar; ½ cup of milk; 1 cup molasses; 1 teaspoonful of butter; 1 tablespoonful of flour; 2 tablespoonfuls of cold water. Boil this mixture 5 minutes; add ½ a cake of Baker's chocolate (grated); boil until it is the consistency of custard; add a pinch of soda; stir well, and remove from the fire. When cold, flavor with vanilla; spread between the layers and on the top of the cake, and set it in a sunny window to dry.

Orange Cake.
Mrs. J. C., Aledo, Ill.

Grated rind of 1 orange; two cups sugar; whites of 4 eggs and yolks of 5; 1 cup sweet milk; 1 cup butter; 2 large teaspoonfuls baking-powder, to be sifted through with the flour; bake quick in jelly-tins. Filling: Take the white of the 1 egg that was left; beat to a frost; add a little sugar, and the juice of the orange; beat together and spread between the layers. If oranges are not to be had, lemons will do instead.

Anxious Mother, Kentland, Ind.

Two-thirds cup of butter; 2 cups sugar; ½ cup sweet milk; 3 cups flour; whites 10 eggs; 3 tablespoonfuls baking-powder. Grate the rind of 2 ordinary-sized oranges into the cake. Press out the juice into the icing. Bake in layers like jelly cake; put the icing between.

Mrs. G. C. S., Rock River Valley.

Two coffee cups white sugar, 2 coffee cups flour, ½ cup cold water, whites of 4 eggs, the yolks of 5 eggs, 2 teaspoonfuls baking-powder; beat yolks and sugar well together, add flour, baking-powder and water, putting in whites of eggs last—beaten well—then take the juice and grated rind of 2 sweet oranges, which, with the exceptions of 1 tablespoon of the juice, I stir in the batter; bake in layers; make frosting of whites of 2 eggs, sugar, and the tablespoon of orange-juice, which place between the layers.

Distress, Cortland, Ill.

Peel the oranges, and chop very fine; to 2 oranges take ½ of a lemon; squeeze the juice and chop the rest; 1 teacup of sugar. Bake a crust as for shortcake; cut open, butter well, and lay the orange between.

Mrs. M. J. T., Chicago.

Three-fourths cup butter; 1¼ cups sugar; four eggs —beaten seperately · 3¼ cups of flour, and 2 heaping teaspoons of baking powder; 1 cup milk. For the frosting. One orange; grate the rind and squeeze the juice and pulp; add ¾ cup of sugar, and then the orange juice. I make 2 cakes of three layers.

Citron Cake.
Mrs. H. S. E., Burlington, Iowa.

Six eggs; 4 cups of flour; 2¼ cups of sugar; 2 cups of citron—cut in little slips; 2 teaspoons baking-powder; 1 cup sweet milk; 1 cup butter.

Ice Cream Cake.
C. A. R., LaCrosse, Wis.

Two cups white sugar, 1 cup butter; 1 cup sweet milk; whites of 8 eggs; 2 teaspoonfuls cream tartar; 1 teaspoonful soda; 3¼ cups winter wheat flour—if spring wheat flour is used, 4 cups. Bake in jelly-pans. Make an icing as follows: 3 cups sugar; 1 of water; boil to a thick clear sirup, and pour boiling hot over the whites of 3 eggs; stir the mixture while pouring in; add 1 teaspoonful citric acid; flavor with lemon or vanilla, and spread each layer and top.

School Cake.
E. L. M., Chicago.

One egg, 1 cup white sugar, 1 cup sweet milk, a piece

of butter the size of an egg, 1 pint flour, into which has been well-sifted 2 teaspoons baking-powder. This cake is good enough for any occasion if made by rule. Work together with butter, sugar, and yolk of the egg till it is light and foamy; add next the milk and flour; then the beaten white of an egg; butter a piece of white paper, and lay in the bottom of the baking-tin; pour in the cake, and bake in a pretty hot oven. It is done when a broom splinter can be inserted and withdrawn clean.

Carlotta's Cup Cake.
Belle, Chicago.

One and a quarter cups sugar; ½ cup butter; ½ cup milk; 1½ teaspoons baking-powder; 3 eggs; 2 cups of flour; nutmeg.

Cottage Cake.
Little Sally, Jefferson, Wis.

Three-fourths of a cup of butter; a cup of white sugar; 1½ cups flour; 4 eggs—yolks and whites beaten seperately; a tablespoonful of sweet milk; 1½ teaspoonfuls of baking powder; lemon and little salt. Rub the baking-powder into the flour.

Scotch Cake.
Leah B., Chicago.

One pound of flour; 1 pound of sugar; 3 eggs; 2 tablespoonfuls of ground cinnamon; ¾ of a pound of butter. Mix the butter with the flour; then add the other ingredients. If not sufficiently stiff to roll, add more flour.

Agnes, Chicago.

Two pounds flour, 1 pound butter, ½ pound powdered sugar; chop flour and butter together, having made butter quite soft by setting near fire. Knead in the sugar. Roll into a sheet not quite ½ inch thick; cut in 2-inch squares. When you want them to look nice put few sugar comfits in center; they will stick by pressing them on with your finger. Bake light brown. Put in stone crock for a few days. They will get soft —just melt in your mouth.

Scotch Currant Bun.
Mrs. W. B. Fyfe, Pontiac, Ill.

Take 1 pint soft yeast; 1 quart lukewarm water; 1

teacupful of shortening, lard and butter; 2 teacupfuls of brown sugar; 1 pound dry currants; 1 pound raisins—cut in two; ¼ pound of citron. Take 6 eggs, beat them and put in allspice, cloves and nutmeg, according to taste. Mix sugar and butter first; then add eggs and fruit; then yeast, water and flour, and mold out into 3 long loaves, as you would do in baking ordinary loaves of bread, taking about the same quantity of flour; then set to rise, which will take about 4 hours; then bake in an ordinary heated oven about 1 hour.

Chocolate and Vanilla Cake.
Gypsy, Ionia, Mich.

One and ½ cups of sugar; 1⅜ cups of flour; ½ cup of butter; 1½ cups of milk; ½ cup of corn-starch; 2 teaspoons of baking powder; the whites of 6 eggs beaten to a froth; 3 teaspoons of vanilla extract; bake in layers, either 2 or 3, and spread frosting between and on the top. Frosting: The whites of 2 eggs, beaten till you can turn the plate bottom side up, and ½ pound pulverized sugar.

Take the yolks of the 8 eggs you have just broken, and make chocolate cake: 1¼ cups sugar (white); ¾ cups butter; 2¼ cups flour; ½ cup milk; the yolks of 8 eggs; 2 teaspoonfuls baking powder; flavor with lemon or vanilla; bake in round pie-tins, in 5 layers; put chocolate frosting between, made in this way: the whites of 3 eggs, beaten very light; ½ pound powdered sugar; ¼ cake of German sweet chocolate; or the same quantity of the bitter.

Cream Puffs.
Gypsy, Ionia, Mich.

Take 2 whole eggs, with 1 cup sugar, ½ cup butter, 1 cup sweet milk, 2 teaspoons baking powder, 2½ cups flour; flavor with lemon. Split the cakes while hot, and fill with cream; ⅔ cup flour; 1 pint milk, 2 eggs; heat the milk; mix sugar, eggs and flour together, and add to the milk; flavor, and cook till like cream.

Cinnamon Cake.
Harmonie, DeKalb, Ill.

One cup sour cream; 1 cup sugar; ½ cup melted

butter; 1 egg; ½ teaspoon soda. Mix as for cookies; roll out and spread ground cinnamon over the top; then roll up as a roll jelly cake, and slice off with a sharp knife and bake. Any good cookey recipe will do.

Jelly Rolls.
Mrs. Ward, Detroit.

Three eggs, ½ a cup of sugar, 1 cup of flour, 1¼ teaspoonfuls of baking powder, the whites of 4 eggs, ⅔ of a cup of pulverized sugar, ½ a cup of flour, ½ a teaspoonful of baking powder, a little salt.

Cocoanut Cake.
Mrs. J. N., Moline, Ill.

One cup of butter beaten to a cream; 3 cups sugar; 3 cups flour; 3 teaspoonfuls of baking powder; ½ cup sweet milk; the whites of 10 eggs; to be baked in layers as jelly cake. Instead of jelly, make a pastry of the whites of 3 eggs and 1 pound of powdered sugar, 1 box of desiccated cocoanut, soaked in milk, and put between the layers.

Ethel, Chicago.

Make a cake as you would for jelly cake, using jelly between the layers—7 or 8 of them. One good, fresh cocoanut; break it, and having peeled it, grate carefully and sprinkle over the top and over the sides thickly. Be sure and make it stick. Also, mix it with sugar before putting it on.

Mrs. Manson, Terre Haute.

Two eggs, 1 cup of white sugar, ½ a cup of sweet milk, ¼ of a cup of butter, 1½ cups of flour, 1½ teaspoonfuls of baking powder. Bake in a moderate oven in pans 1 inch deep.

To prepare the desiccated cocoanut, beat the whites of 2 eggs to a stiff froth; add 1 cup of puverized sugar and the cocoanut, after soaking it in boiling milk. Spread the mixture between the layers of cake and over the top.

Betsey Trotwood, Westville, Ind.

Whites of 12 eggs; 1¼ pounds of butter; 2 cups of pulverized sugar. Bake as for jelly cake. Then take the whites of 4 eggs, ½ pound cocoanut, 1 cup sugar;

for the upper cake add cocoanut before baking. For frosting, take 2 eggs and 1 cup of sugar. Do not beat the eggs for frost.

Citron Cake.
Agnes, Chicago.

Four eggs well beaten; 1¼ pounds sugar; ¾ pound butter; 1 pint sweet milk; 1½ pounds flour; ¼ pound citron. Cut in thin pieces, well floured; baking powder as usual.

Cream Cake.
P. P. C., Chicago.

Two tablespoons butter; 2 teacups sugar; 3 eggs; ½ teacup sweet milk; 2 tablespoons cold water; 2 teacups flour; 2 teaspoons of baking powder; bake quickly on 3 or 4 round tins. The "cream" for same is ½ pint milk; ½ teacup sugar; small piece of butter; 1 egg; 1 tablespoon of corn-starch. Boil until very thick; when nearly cold, flavor with vanilla; when the cakes are cool, put them together with it.

Gold and Silver Cake.
P. P. C., Chicago.

One teacup white sugar; ½ teacup butter; whites of 4 eggs; ⅜ teacup sweet milk; 2 teacups flour; 2 teaspoons baking powder; flavor.

Gold cake: Same as above, using the yolks of the 4 eggs, and adding 1 whole egg.

Currant Cake.
P. P. C. Chicago.

One-half cup butter; 1 of sugar; 2 eggs; ½ cup milk; 1½ cups flour; 1½ teaspoons baking powder; 1 cup well washed currants, stirred in the last thing.

Buffalo Cream Cake.
J. V. C., Elgin, Ill.

One egg; 1 cup sugar; 1 tablespoonful butter; ⅔ cup milk; 1 teaspoonful baking powder; 1 teaspoonful vanilla; 1⅔ cup flour; salt, and bake as for jelly cake, in 3 layers.

Cream for above: Heat 1 pint of milk, and add to it 1 tablespoonful of corn-starch dissolved in a little milk; 2 eggs; 1 cup sugar, all beaten together; boil it until it thickens. Split the cake when cold and fill with cream.

Cream Cake,
Mrs. Geo. C., Chicago.

One cup white sugar; 1½ cups flour; 3 eggs beaten separate and very light; 2 tablespoons water; 1 teaspoon baking powder. Bake in 2 cakes. Cream: One pint milk; 1 cup sugar; ½ cup butter; 3 eggs; 2 tablespoons flour; lemon extract. Cut each cake and fill with the cream.

Marble Spice Cake.
Birdie K., Chicago.

Three-quarters of a pound of flour, well dried; 1 pound of white sugar; ¼ pound of butter; whites of 14 eggs; 1 tablespoonful of cream of tartar mixed with the flour. When the cake is mixed, take out about a teacup of batter and stir into it 1 teaspoonful of cinnamon, 1 of mace, 1 of cloves, 2 of spice and 1 of nutmeg. Fill your mold about an inch deep with the white batter, and drop into this, in several places, a spoonful of the dark mixture. Then put in another layer of white, and add the dark as before. Repeat this until your batter is used up. This makes 1 large cake.

Lemon Cake.
Evaline, Goodland, Ind.

Three cups of sugar, 1 of butter, 1 of milk, 4 of flour. 5 eggs; stir the butter and eggs to a cream; beat the eggs separately, the whites to a stiff froth; dissolve a little soda in the milk; mix altogether; sift the flour and put in by degrees, and add the juice and grated rind of a fresh lemon.

Florence, Valparaiso, Ind.

Twelve eggs; 1½ pounds sugar; ¾ pound flour; grate the outside of 2 lemons with the inside of 1; or add 1 glass of wine, with 3 teaspoonfuls of essence of lemon.

Lemon Jelly Cake.
Hattie, Aurora, Ill.

Two cups of sugar; ¾ of a cup of butter; 1 cup of milk; 3 cups of flour; 2 teaspoons of baking-powder;

4 eggs. Bake in layers. Jelly: Take two lemons; pulp and peel; 1 coffee cup of sugar; piece of butter size of an egg; and 2 eggs. Mix and boil till clear.

Lemon Layer Cake.
E. O. G., Chicago.

Two cups sugar; ½ cup butter; 1 cup milk; 3 cups flour; 3 eggs; two teaspoons baking-powder. Jelly: 1 cup sugar; 1 egg; 1 tablespoon butter; the grated rind and juice of 1 lemon, all boiled till thick.

Ice Cream Cake.
Mrs. Lofty, Chicago.

One cup of sugar; 2 eggs; ½ cup of sweet milk; 1½ cups of flour; piece of butter the size of an egg; 3 teaspoons baking-powder. Cream for cake: ½ cup of sweet milk; 3 teaspoons of powdered sugar; 1 tablespoon of corn-starch; boil until thick; flavor with vanilla.

Chocolate Cake.
Mrs. G. G., Champaign, Ill.

One cup butter, 2 cups sugar, 1 cup sweet milk, 5 eggs, 3½ cups flour, 3½ teaspoonfuls baking-powder. Save out the white of 1 egg for frosting; flavor with vanilla; bake in 4 thick layers.

Frosting: 1 cup of sugar; water enough to dissolve; boil till *very thick;* while hot, pour over the beaten white of one egg, and at the same time stir briskly till thick; add 2 sticks of German sweet chocolate grated fine, and spread over cake immediately. Have all the cakes baked so the frosting can be used as soon as made, for it hardens very quickly.

A Mother, Illinois.

Two cups sugar; ⅔ cup of butter; 1 cup sweet milk; 3 cups flour; 3 eggs; two teaspoons baking-powder; lemon extract. Bake as jelly-cake.

Caramel: The whites of 3 eggs beaten very stiff; 2 cups sugar boiled until almost candy; pour very slowly on the whites, beating them quite fast; ½ cake Baker's chocolate grated; vanilla extract; stir until cool, then put between each cake and over the top and sides.

Mrs. H., Odell, Ill.

One cup of sugar; ⅔ cup of sweet milk; 1 egg; 1⅞ cups of flour; 1 tablespoonful of butter; 2 teaspoons of baking-powder. Make this in four cakes. Mixture to put between: To the white of 1 egg add 2 tablespoons of sugar, 2 of grated chocolate. I use the sweet chocolate. Put this quantity between each layer, and also on the top. You will find it very nice.

Fig Cake.
Evaline, Goodland, Ind.

For the cake take 1 cup of butter, 2 cups of sugar, 3½ cups of flour, ½ cup of sweet milk, whites of 7 eggs, 2 teaspoons of baking powder. Bake in layers. For the filling, take a pound of figs; chop fine, and put in a stewpan on the stove; pour over it a teacup of water, and add ½ cup of sugar. Cook all together until soft and smooth. Let it cook, and spread between the layers.

Marble Cake.
Aunt Lucy, Chicago.

Light: White sugar, 1½ cups; butter, ½ cup; sweet milk, ½ cup; flour, 2½ cups; whites of 4 eggs; 2 teaspoons of baking powder; flavor with lemons or almons. Dark part: Brown sugar, 1 cup; molasses, ½ cup; butter, ½ cup; sweet milk, ½ cup; yolks of 4 eggs; 2½ cups of flour; 2 teaspoons of baking powder; mix in separate pans; flavor with spices.

Pork Fruit Cake.
Evaline, Goodland, Ind.

One pound pork chopped fine; 1 pint boiling water; 1 cup sugar, 2 of molasses; 1 pound raisins; ¼ pound of citron; 1 nutmeg; 2 tablespoons of cloves, 3 of cinnamon, 1 of soda; 1 teaspoon of ginger; and 4 cups of flour.

Pork Cake.
Gretchen, Rockford, Ill.

Three-quarters of a pound of salt pork, chopped as fine as lard; then pour on a pint of boiling, strong coffee; 2 cups brown sugar, 1 of molasses; 2 teaspoonfuls cloves, 1 of cinnamon, 1 nutmeg; 2 teaspoonfuls of soda; 1½ pounds raisins; also citron and currants; bake slowly. This will make 3 cakes.

Nut Cake.
Agnes, Chicago.

Two cups sugar; 1 of butter; 3 of flour; 1 of cold water; 4 eggs; baking powder; 1½ cups kernels of hickory or white walnuts.

Ethel, Amboy.

One cup butter; 2 of white sugar; 4 of flour; 1 of sweet milk; 8 eggs, the whites; 3 teaspoonfuls of baking powder; 2 cups hickory nuts, picked out of the shells, and cut up with a clean knife.

Tea Cake.
Agnes, Chicago.

One cup sugar; 1½ cups butter; 1 cup flour; 4 eggs; beaten separately; 1½ teaspoons of baking powder; add raisins if you like. Is almost as good as pound-cake.

Bertha Corlyle, Hyde Park.

One cup of sugar; 1 tablespoonful of butter; 3 eggs; beat well together; then add a cup of sweet milk (you may use part water), and a quart of sifted flour, into which you have mixed a spoonful of cream of tartar, and ½ a teaspoonful of soda; bake in a quick oven. It is improved by sprinkling sugar over the top (before baking). This will make 2 cakes, which are best when eaten warm

FROSTING, ICING, ETC.

Frosting.
German American, Chicago.

BEAT ¼ pound pulverized sugar with the juice of 1 large lemon; add the white of 1 egg beaten to a stiff froth; and 1 tablespoon of rum or arrak. Beat till a snowy white, put over your cake and dry in a warm oven.

Chocolate Frosting.
Sarah E., Chicago.

One cake (or ¼ pound) Maillard's French vanilla sweet chocolate, grated; ½ cup granulated sugar; ¾ cup sweet milk; 1 tablespoon butter; a little salt. Boil 20 minutes, stirring constantly. Take from the fire and pour into a dish. When near cool, add 1 tablespoon of vanilla; spread on the cake. If the mixture is thicker than jelly, thin it with milk. This quantity will ice 2 cakes, 3 layers each. The best cake is gold cake baked in jelly-tins. This will prove a success if the experimenter can catch that "twist of the wrist" that forms an essential but indefinable part of every woman's recipe.

Aunt Polly, Chicago.

Whites of 3 eggs, beaten very light; 9 tablespoonfuls of powdered sugar, and 6 tablespoons of grated chocolate.

Mrs. Knowlton, Rockford.

First make a cream or custard pie, reserving for frosting the whites of 3 eggs, using the yolks and 1 or 2 whole eggs for the pie. While your pie is baking scrape very fine 2 tablespoonfuls of Baker's chocolate, and place it on the back part of the stove to melt. Now beat the whites of your eggs well; add 6 teaspoonfuls of pulverized sugar. When the chocolate is melted, stir a little of the frosting into it, beating very hard; add a little more, until all is added. Do not make the mistake of stirring the chocolate into the egg, as it will remain clouded. When the pie is done, pour the frosting on top, and return to the oven for 5 minutes. I find in using chocolate it is much better to warm it until it is soft enough to mix in frosting or Charlotte Russe, than to dissolve it with water.

Icing.
Yankee Hoosier, Lafayette, Ind.

Two and a half cups sugar, ⅔ cup water; boil together until it candies; then add the whites of 3 eggs, slightly beaten, stirring briskly for 15 minutes, or until it seems perfectly smooth and white; then add the juice of 1 lemon. This is sufficient for one large white mountain cake, of 8 or 9 layers, covering also top and sides.

Mrs. Rose B., Addison.

Beat the whites of 4 eggs with 1 pound of powdered sugar sifted, with ½ a tablespoon starch, and ¼ of an ounce of fine gum-arabic. Stir it well.

Chocolate Icing.
Evaline, Goodland, Ind.

Take the whites of two eggs, 1½ cups powdered sugar and 6 large tablespoons of chocolate.

Chocolate Filling.
Heatherbell, Detroit.

Whites of 3 eggs; 1½ teacups of sugar; 3 tablespoonfuls grated chocolate; 1 teaspoonful vanilla. Beat the whites of the eggs well, and then add the other ingredients; then beat all together and spread between the layers and on top of cake.

PIES.

Mock Mince Pie.
Sky-Blue Cardinal, Chicago.

SIX soda crackers rolled fine; 1 cup hot water; 1 cup molasses; ½ cup brown sugar; ¼ cup vinegar; ½ cup melted butter; 1 cup raisins chopped; 1 teaspoon each of cinnamon, cloves, allspice and nutmeg. Measure in a coffee-cup.

Mrs. M. Coldwater, Mich.

Three soda crackers rolled fine, 1 cup of cold water, 1 cup of molasses, ½ cup of brown sugar, ¼ cup of sour cider or vinegar, ¼ cup of melted butter, ½ cup of raisins, ½ cup of currants, 1 egg beaten light, 1 teaspoon of cinnamon, ¼ teaspoon each of cloves, allspice and nutmeg, 5 apples chopped fine.

English Mince Pie.
Mrs. Louisa T., Chicago.

Three and a half pounds each of beef and suet chopped fine; 3½ pounds each of raisins and currants; 7 pounds of apples chopped; 1 pound of candied citron; 2 pounds of sugar; 1 ounce of nutmeg; 4 quarts of good cider; 1 pint of best vinegar; salt; and a pint of golden sirup. Half the raisins should be stoned and chopped, the other ½ left whole.

Pie Crust.
Aunt Lucy, Chicago.

Take 3 cups of sifted flour, 1 cup of lard, a little salt, and ½ a cup of cold water. Handle as little as possible. Never butter or grease your pie pans—it will make the under crust stick and the pie hard to slip out.

Lemon Pie.
Aunt Sally, Springfield, O.

Yolks of 2 eggs; 1 cup of sugar; the juice and grated

COOKERY—PIES. 93

rind of 1 lemon; 1½ cups of cold water; two tablespoonfuls of flour, and 5 of water mixed for thickening. Bake until done, but not watery. Beat the whites of the eggs to a stiff froth and stir in ¾ cup of sugar. Spread over the top and brown in the oven.

Pansy, St. Joseph, Mich.

Two lemons; grate off the outer peel; chop the rest very fine; put 2 tablespoons of corn-starch in 1 teacup of hot water, and boil; when cool add 2 teacups of white sugar; the beaten yolks of 4 eggs; then add the chopped peel and the juice; stir well together; bake till the crust is done—only 1 crust; beat the whites of the 4 eggs to a stiff froth; add 5 spoons (table) of sugar, stirring in well; pour over the pie while hot; set in the oven to brown.

Jennie Dean, St. Paul.

Two large fresh lemons; grate off the rind; if not bitter, reserve it for the filling of the pie; pare off every bit of the white skin of the lemon (as it toughens while cooking); then cut the lemon into very thin slices with sharp knife, and take out the seeds; 2 cupfuls of sugar, 3 tablespoonfuls of water, and 2 of sifted flour. Put into the pie a layer of lemon, then 1 of sugar, then 1 of the grated rind, and, lastly, of flour, and so on till the ingredients are used; sprinkle the water over all, and cover with upper crust. Be sure to have the under crust lap over the upper, and pinch it well, as the sirup will cook all out if care is not taken when finishing the edge of crust. This quantity makes 1 medium-sized pie.

Orange Pie.
Martha, Galva, Ill.

Take the juice and grated rind of 1 orange; 1 small cup of sugar; yolks of 3 eggs; 1 tablespoon of corn-starch, made smooth with milk; piece of butter as large as a chestnut, and 1 cup of milk. Beat the whites of the 3 eggs with sugar, and place on the top after the pie is baked—leaving in the oven until browned.

Another.—Grate the rind of a large, sweet orange; squeeze the juice and press off the pulp, picking out the seeds. Cream, ¼ of a cup (or butter), ½ cup of sugar, 1 egg beaten light, 1 tablespoon of flour rubbed smooth in ¼ cup of water. Stir in the orange, and bake with 2 crusts. In this, as indeed in all cooking, judgment must be used, as oranges vary in size and sweetness; but these are the usual proportions, and are sufficient for an ordinary-sized pie.

Mrs. J. C. H., Chicago.

Take 4 good-sized oranges, peel, seed, and cut in very small pieces. Add a cup of sugar, and let stand. Into a quart of nearly boiling milk stir 2 tablespoonfuls of corn-starch mixed with a little water, and the yolks of 3 eggs. When this is done, let it cool, then mix with the oranges. Put it in simply a lower crust. Make a frosting of the whites of the eggs and ½ cup sugar. Spread it over top of pies, and place for a few seconds in the oven to brown.

Mother's Lemon Pie.
Lillie W., Englewood, Ill.

Juice and grated rind of 1 lemon; 1 cup white sugar; 1 tablespoonful of butter; 2 tablespoonfuls sweet milk; 4 eggs. Mix it all as carefully and thoroughly as for a cake. If the mixture is not sufficient to fill your pie-plate, add more milk. If you want it superexcellent, beat the whites of 2 eggs with 2 tablespoonfuls of powdered sugar for a miringue; spread it on smoothly after the pie is baked, and set back into the oven to brown slightly.

Two-Crust Lemon Pie.
C. M. W., Hudson, Mich.

Line your pie-dish with a good crust; roll your lemons to soften them; grate the rind of one large, or two small lemons; cut the lemons in thin slices; pick out the seeds; spread evenly one layer over the crust; spread 1 cup of sugar over the lemon; then add 1 cup of paste, made by taking 4 tablespoons of flour, wetting it with cold water the same as you would to make starch; turn boiling water on it, stirring while cooking on the stove a few moments, adding a pinch of salt with the grated rind of the lemons. When thickened enough pour it over the sugar and lemon; cover with a crust, cutting slits in to let out the air; bake slowly.

Squash Pie.
Germania, South Evanston.

Obtain a good Hubbard squash, saw into quarters, and bake 2 of these until dry and thoroughly done. Scoop out the dry mealy part, and while warm add a tablespoonful of flour, and rub it well, wetting as you go with a little milk. This should be heated, and to this quantity of squash you will want 3 pints of milk. Now come the eggs; 2 for a pie will do; 3 won't hurt. Use a small teacup of sugar for each pie. To this add the yolks of the eggs, and beat a long time, adding for each pie one teaspoonful of ginger and one of cinnamon. Line your tins with a nice paste, in which you have sifted a little baking-powder. Beat up your whites to a stiff froth; stir the yolks in first, then the whites; fill your shell and place in oven, which must not be too hot, as they will brown too fast and spoil the golden foam that comes to the top.

Eloise Howe, Rockford, Ill.

Boil enough squash with a little salt in the water to make a quart of pulp; 1 quart of milk; 2 cups of sugar; 1 tablespoon ginger; ½ a nutmeg the grated rind of a lemon; four eggs, or 2 with corn-starch; bake in deep pie-plates.

R., Dubuque, Iowa.

Steam a fine Hubbard squash; when done beat perfectly smooth; add 2 eggs, ½ cup butter, 1 quart rich cream; sugar to taste; flavor with nutmeg or grated lemon. This makes three pies.

Polly Snooks, Chicago.

Steam the squash over a pot of corn-beef until it is well done; then mash fine, adding 2 eggs well beaten to each pie. It requires a good deal of sugar to make them nice, some salt, very little pepper, and enough ginger to make it quite strong. Thin with milk and cream mixed together, or milk alone, will make good pies. Bake without top crust, quite brown.

Squash Without Crust.
Mary Moore, Chicago.

Pare the stewed squash in the ordinary way. Then grease the plates (I use earthen ones) and sift corn-meal over them until evenly covered with a thin layer. It must not be too thick, and must have no breaks in it. Pour the prepared squash into the plates gently, so as not to disturb the meal; bake thoroughly, and cut when cold. Use pumpkin in the same way. It is quickly prepared, economical, healthy and palatable.

Pumpkin Pie.
Aunt Lucy, Chicago.

Pare and cut in small bits, and boil the day before pies are made; when tender rub through the collander; then add to about 3 pints of the strained pumpkin 5 eggs, a little salt, a pint of sweet milk; sweeten to taste; a little ginger and lemon extract for flavoring; bake in a quick oven. With this, use "Aunt Lucy's" crust, above given.

Mrs. John T. B., Quincy.

Take equal parts stewed pumpkin and rich sweet milk. To a quart of the mixture add 3 well-beaten eggs, a teacup of sugar, and ½ a nutmeg grated. Line a deep pan with crust, set in the oven and fill full; some like a pinch of salt added to each pie.

Fruit Pie.
Mrs. W. K. M., Green Bay, Wis.

Line a soup plate with a rich paste, and spread with a layer of strawberry or raspberry preserves; over which sprinkle 2 tablespoonfuls of finely chopped almonds (blanched of course) and ¼ ounce of candied lemon peel cut into shreds. Then mix the following ingredients: ¼ pound white sugar; ¼ pound butter, melted; 4 yolks and 2 whites of eggs, and a few drops of almond essence. Beat well together and pour the mixture into the soup plate over the preserves, etc. Bake in a moderately-warm oven. When cold sprinkle or sift a little powdered sugar over the top. A little cream eaten with it is a great addition.

Washington Pie.
Mrs. George M., Adrian, Mich.

For the crust use 2 cups sugar, ½ cup butter, 3 cups sifted flour, 4 eggs, ½ teaspoonful cream tartar. For the filling: 1 tablespoonful corn-starch, boiled in ½ pint milk; beat the yolk 1 egg very light, and stir into the milk, flavor with vanilla, and when cold add the other half of the milk and the white of the egg beaten to a stiff froth and stirred in quickly; spread this between the cakes, and ice it with the white of 1 egg and 8 tablespoonfuls of fine sifted sugar flavored with lemon.

Marlborough Pie.
Roxcy, Maywood, Ill.

Six tart apples; 6 ounces of sugar; 6 ounces of butter or thick cream; 6 eggs; the grated peel of 1 lemon, and ½ the juice. Grate the apples, after paring and coreing them; stir together the butter and sugar, as for cake. Then add the other ingredients, and bake in rich under-paste only.

Potato Pie.
Cora Lee, Bloomington.

Potato pie is made the same as pumpkin pie: Cook and mash the potatoes; then put in an egg to a pie; thin out with milk, sweeten and flavor to taste.

Mrs. N. W. H., Chicago.

Pare and grate 1 large white potato into a deep dish; add the grated rind and juice of 1 lemon; the white of 1 egg well beaten; 1 teacup of cold water; 1 teacup of white sugar. Pour this into a plate lined with a nice crust and bake. When done have ready the whites of 3 eggs, well beaten, with ½ cup of powdered sugar and a few drops of lemon extract. Pour this over the pie and return to the oven till of a rich brown color. When cool enough a small spoonful of jelly may be put over the pie.

Sweet Potato Pie.
Aunt Lucy, Chicago.

Scrape clean 2 good-sized sweet potatoes; boil; when tender rub through the collander; beat the yolks of 3 eggs light; stir with a pint of sweet milk into the potato; add a small teacup of sugar, a pinch of salt; flavor with a little fresh lemon, or extract will do; bake as you do your pumpkin pies; when done make a meringue top with the whites of eggs and powdered sugar; brown a moment in the oven.

Mince Pie.
Lena Gray, Chicago.

Seven pounds beef, after it is boiled and chopped; 7 pounds apples; 6 pounds raisins; 4 pounds currants; 6½ pounds sugar; 1 pint molasses; 1 pound suet; a little salt; four large oranges; cinnamon, cloves, mace, allspice and nutmeg to your taste; 2 pounds citron; 3 gallons cider. Boil the orange-peel in some of the cider to make it soft; use the cider the peel was boiled in also. If I dared, I'd say put in a teacup of brandy when you are ready to bake.

Mincemeat.
Aunt Lucy, Chicago.

Four pounds meat, 3 pounds suet, 3 pounds raisins, 3 pounds currants, 1 pound citron, 3 pounds brown sugar, 1 pint sirup or molasses, grated rind and juice of 8 lemons, 2 ounces ground cinnamon, 1 ounce of cloves, 1 ounce of nutmeg. Boil meat very tender; pick out all bits of fat and gristle. Chop the suet fine, removing all strings and threads; then mix thoroughly together; season with salt and black pepper; wash many times the currants; let them well dry, and then add to the mixture; seed the raisins, and chop not fine; add the sirup and spices; slice the citron thin. To a quart of the above add a pint of chopped apples. It is best only to add the apples at each baking. Wet with sweet cider till the mixture is juicy. When ready to bake, take mincemeat, just enough for the number of pies wanted; place it on the stove in a crock or jar and let it get heated through; taste and add whatever you think it needs—it may be a little salt or spice, or perhaps it is not sweet enough. Make pastry rich; place the mincemeat in the pie, not too full; and some little bits of butter, a few whole raisins, and a few slices of citron. Keep mincemeat well covered and in a cool place.

Maggie M. W., Chicago.

Three bowls of meat; 5 bowls of apples; 1 bowl of molasses; 1 of vinegar; 1 of cider; 1 of suet or butter; 2 of raisins; 5 of sugar; 1 bottle of brandy, or, if you prefer, leave out the brandy and add more cider; 2 tablespoonfuls each of cinnamon, nutmeg and cloves;

1 tablespoonful each of salt and black pepper; 3 lemons—grate in the outside and squeeze in the juice. Add all but the meat and spices; boil until the raisins are tender, and pour on to the meat and spices; add brandy after it is cold. If suet is used, scald it. This makes a large quantity, but it is very nice and keeps well.

Aunt D., Chicago

Boil 1 pound ox tongue or fresh beef tender; then add 2 pounds beef suet, chopped fine; 2 pounds stoned raisins, 2 pounds currants, 2 pounds good apples, 2½ pounds fine sugar, ½ or ¾ pound candied orange, lemon, and citron; the grated rind 2 large lemons, 2 nutmegs, dessert spoonful salt, teaspoonful powdered mace, same powdered ginger, and ½ pint best sirup. Press closely into jars, and keep well covered. In a few days it will be fit to use.

Custard Pie.
A. B. C., Chicago.

Take about ½ pint of flour, a pinch of salt, lard the size of an egg, and rub together with the hands, not too fine if you want it flaky; use just enough cold water to stick together. Do not knead or work it much. Line a pie-tin with crust, and bake. If it rises up while baking, press it down with your hand before it gets hard. Heat 1 pint of milk boiling hot; then take ½ cup of flour ½ cup of sugar and the yolks of two eggs. Beat them together, and stir into the boiling milk, and cook about 5 minutes, (I cook in a 3-pint basin, set in another dish containing water, to prevent burning). After the crust is baked, put in the mixture; then put upon the top a frosting made of the whites of the eggs, and 2 tablespoons of sugar, and brown in the oven. Flavor with lemon. To be eaten cold.

Cinnamon Pie.
Mrs. Fernando, Chicago.

One pound brown sugar, 2 ounces cinnamon, ½ cupful butter; divide in 3 parts; mix 2 eggs and 1½ cupfuls milk together; for the crust take 4 cupfuls flour, 1¼ cupfuls lard or butter, 2 heaping teaspoonfuls baking powder, salt to taste; mix with milk sufficient to make soft dough; divide in three parts and roll thin. Put 1 layer of crust in a deep pie-dish and cover it with sugar, then cinnamon, and a small piece of butter; then wet with the mixture of milk and egg, saving enough for the other two parts; lay the 2d and 3d crusts on and do the same as with the first; there should be no crust on top. Bake in a quick oven.

Cream Pie.
Cricket, Chicago.

Bake a crust in a large pie-pan; lift it out on a plate; for filling, take 1 pint of very rich milk; boil ¾ of it; with the remaining ¼ stir 2 tablespoonfuls of cornstarch; add to the boiling milk, stirring all the time; then add ½ tea-cup of sugar; then the yolks of 2 eggs, well beaten and thinned with a little milk. Remove from the fire; flavor with vanilla and nutmeg, and pour into the crust. Whip the whites; add ½ teacup sugar; frost the pie, and place in the oven to brown slightly. Serve cold.

Mrs. J. M. T., Chicago.

One large tablespoon of butter; 3 of sugar; 2 of flour; 2 eggs, and a little more than ½ pint of milk. Beat the sugar and butter to a cream. Beat the eggs well, and mix them with the milk, then stir in the flour, etc. Flavor with whatever you like—if with lemon, grate the rind and use some essence. This is for 1 pie.

Constant Reader, North Point, Md.

Place 1 pint of milk in tea-kettle boiler until hot (not boiling); add one cup white sugar, ½ cup flour, and 2 eggs, well beaten; stir rapidly until thoroughly cooked; flavor with lemon or vanilla; pour over crust, which should be previously baked. Beat the white of 2 eggs to a stiff froth; add 3 tablespoons of powdered sugar; pour over the custard; set in oven, and allow to come to light brown. To be eaten cold.

Millie Millett, Canton, Ill.

Roll the crust to a medium thickness; take a good-sized tablespoonful of flour; mix with a ½ cup of sugar; a piece of butter the size of a hickory nut; ½ teaspoonful extract of lemon; coffeecup of good rich cream. Bake as you would a custard. This is to be eaten the day it is baked.

Cocoanut Pie.
Mrs. E. K., Blue Island, Ill.

I put a cup of cocoanut to soak in sweet milk as early in the morning as I can. I take a teacup of the cocoanut and put it into a coffeecup, and fill up with milk. When ready to bake I take 2 tablespoonfuls of flour, mix with milk, and stir in ¾ of a cup of milk (or water), place on the stove, and stir until it thickens. Add butter the size of a walnut while warm. When cool add a little salt, 2 eggs, saving out the white of one for the top. Sweeten to taste. Add the cocoanut, beating well. Fill the crust and bake. When done, have the extra white beaten ready to spread over the top. Return to the oven and brown lightly.

Winnifred, Warsaw, Ill.

Open the eyes of a cocoanut with a pointed knife or a gimlet, and pour out the milk into a cup; then break the shell and take out the meat and grate it fine. Take the same weight of sugar and the grated nut and stir together; beat 4 eggs, the whites and yolks separately to a stiff foam; mix 1 cup of cream, and the milk of the cocoanut with the sugar and nut, then add the eggs and a few drops of orange or lemon extract. Line deep pie-tins with a nice crust, fill them with the custard, and bake carefully ½ an hour.

PUDDINGS.

Suet Pudding.
Schoolmarm Marseilles, Ill.

ONE cup of suet, chopped fine; 1 teacup of molasses; 1 teacup of sweet milk; 3½ teacups of flour; 1 cup of raisins; 1 teaspoon of soda. Steam 2 hours. Sauce for the same: 1 cup of sugar; ¼ cup of butter; 1 egg; 1 tablespoon of vinegar; 1 teaspoon of lemon extract. Beat well, and bring to a boil. Serve hot.

Gypsy, Chicago.

One cup of suet, 2½ of flour, 1 of raisins, 1 of currants; a small cup of molasses; spice to taste; 1 dessert-spoonful of baking powder. Bake ¾ of an hour.

Dallas, Chicago.

One pint of bread sponge; 1 cup chopped suet; 1 cup brown sugar; 1 cup sweet milk; 1 large cup raisins; 1½ teaspoons cinnamon; 1 of cloves; 1 of salt; 1½ teaspoons soda; flour to make very stiff. Put in a 2-quart pan, and steam 2½ hours. Do not lift the cover until done. Make any kind of sauce you like best, and serve hot.

Bread Pudding.
Susan, Princeton.

One coffee cup bread crumbs, dried and rolled fine. 1 teacup of sugar; 1 quart of milk; 1 teaspoonful ginger; a little salt; 3 eggs (saving out the whites of 2); When baked, spread jelly over the top; then a frosting made of the whites of the eggs, and 1 tablespoonful of sugar. Return to the oven until slightly browned.

Theo. C. C., Chicago.

Soak your bread in as little cold water as will soak it thoroughly; then beat it up, water and all, and add flour enough to make it the consistency of apple sauce; add sugar, cinnamon, a little nutmeg, allspice, which must predominate, and some well-washed currants; also a little butter melted and stirred in. If it is baker's bread, scald a little saleratus, and stir in thoroughly, but, if it is house-made bread, add a teaspoonful of baking powder to your flour, at the rate of 2 teaspoonfuls to a quart of pudding. Bake in shallow pans; cut in squares when serving; turn over, and put on each a small piece of butter, and dust plentifully with powdered sugar. This requires a little care in making, but is universally liked and very wholesome and economical, as no eggs or cream are required.

Mrs. W. A. S., Arlington, Ill.

Of clean, broken pieces, a quart when crumbed—I put sweet milk to them right after breakfast, and set them on the open top of the boiling teakettle. They will swell and soften so as to nearly soak up the milk by the middle of the forenoon. Then beat up 3 eggs and add them, also 1 teacup of sugar, 1 teaspoonful of ground cinnamon, and a $\frac{1}{2}$ teaspoonful of ground cloves, a little grated nutmeg, a tablespoonful of butter, and $\frac{2}{3}$ of a pint of raisins, the latter picked over carefully and washed by pouring boiling water over them. The boiling water softens them and causes them to swell. Mix all ingredients together thoroughly, and bake about an hour in a moderately-heated oven. It can be sliced and eaten cold with a relish, or eaten while warm with sweet sauce.

Rena's Pudding.

Agnes, Chicago.

Take stale bread; place in a pan; cover with cold water; set on back of stove—not too hot a place. If bread is sour, put a little soda in water; let soak until soft. If you have more water on the bread than it takes up, pour it off until dry; then beat fine with a spoon; if it is very watery, press water out and throw away. To 1 quart of bread, after soaked, add 1 cup (large) of currants or raisins; 1 large tablespoon of sugar. Bake in hot oven for 40 minutes, if not too large. Eat with cream or milk, flavored and sweetened, thin boiled custard, or sugar and butter.

Imitation Plum Pudding.
J. C. S., Chicago.

Soak some dried apples all night; in the morning chop very fine; put a teacupful of them into a pint of molasses, and keep slightly warm for an hour or 2; after that add 1 cup of chopped suet, 1 of water, 1 of chopped raisins, a pinch of salt, a teaspoonful of cinnamon, 3 pints of flour, and 2 teaspoonfuls of baking powder. Put the flour in last, and stir all together thoroughly. Boil 2½ hours in a bowl or tin pudding mold. This may be eaten with wine sauce, and is a good imitation of genuine plum pudding.

Bread and Apple Pudding.
S. A. T., Champaign.

Butter a pudding dish; place in it alternate layers of bread crumbs and thinly sliced apples; sprinkle sugar over each layer of apples; when the dish is filled, let the top layer be of bread crumbs, over which 2 or 3 tablespoonfuls of melted butter should be poured. Bake in a moderately hot oven, and place 2 or 3 nails under the pudding dish to keep from burning in the bottom; let it bake from ¾ to a whole hour, according to the quality of the cooking apples.

Rice Pudding.
Jennie, LaPorte, Ind.

Soak 1 cupful of best rice; after soaking 4 hours, drain it off; place the rice in pudding dish; add 1 cupful sugar, and 1 teaspoonful salt, and 11 cupfuls milk and spice; put in a moderate oven, and bake from 2 to 3 hours, stirring occasionally at first if the rice settles.

Mrs. E., Kalamazoo.

Take a cup of rice, place in an earthen dish, pour over it 1 pint of fresh milk; allow it to cook slowly until the rice is soft enough to eat; then pour over a pint of cold milk; add pinch of salt. Take the yolks of 4 eggs and beat in smooth 4 tablespoons of powdered sugar, and 1 teaspoon of vanilla; stir well into the rice. Place in a brisk oven. After allowing it to come to a light brown, place on the top the whites of the 4 eggs, beaten to a stiff froth, and 4 tablespoons of powdered sugar. Allow this also to come to a delicate brown; set in a cool place, the colder the better. It is very nice eaten with oranges cut in slices.

Susan, Princeton.

One teacup of rice; 1 teacup of sugar; 1 quart milk, 1 teaspoonful cinnamon; raisins if you please. Bake slowly 1½ hours.

Twenty-six Summers, Coldwater, Mich.

(To be eaten cold). One and a ½ teacups of rice (boiled until soft); stir in ½ pint of milk, sugar, salt, and the yolks of 3 eggs. Boil up or bake just enough to warm through. Beat the whites of 3 eggs for frosting, seasoned with vanilla, or lemon if preferred, and spread over the top of the pudding when done. Return it to the oven just long enough to bake the frosting.

Apple Pudding.
Mrs. Henry C. Port Huron.

Make a good paste; roll it out and place in a basin rubbed with dripping; press out the plaits so that the crust may be of an equal thickness all round; peel and cut up 4 large apples, put ½ of them in, then add 1 tablespoonful moist sugar and 1 of cloves; put in the rest of the apples; cover the top well over with paste, press it down, that the water may not get in; tie a cloth over; put it into boiling water and boil fast for 2½ hours, if the crust be made of dripping, and an hour longer if it be made of suet; take off the cloth, pass a knife around the edge of the basin. Turn out the pudding carefully when sending it to table.

Tapioca Pudding.
Teutonia, Wis.

No. 1—Soak 8 tablespoonfuls of tapioca in a quart of warm milk till soft; then add 2 tablespoonfuls of melted butter; 5 eggs well beaten; cinnamon and sugar to your taste; bake in a buttered dish without any lining. No. 2—Put a teacup of tapioca and a teaspoonful of salt into a pint and a ½ of water, and let them stand 5 hours where they will be kept warm. Two hours before dinner pare and core 6 apples; place in a pudding dish, and fill the holes with sugar, over which sprinkle cinnamon; add a teacup of water, and bake 1 hour, turning the apples to prevent drying. When the apples are soft, pour over them the tapioca and bake an hour. Serve with hard sauce of butter and sugar.

E. L. M., Chicago.

Boil ½ a teacup of tapioca in ½ a pint of water till it melts. By degrees stir in ½ a pint of milk and boil till the tapioca is very thick. Add a well beaten egg, sugar, and flavoring to taste. Turn into your pudding dish and cook gently in the oven ¾ of an hour. This dish is excellent for delicate children.

Mrs. T. W., Fairbury, Ill

Four tablespoonfuls of tapioca; 1 quart of milk; 4 eggs, leaving out the whites of 2 for frosting; 3 tablespoonfuls of sugar. Soak the tapioca over night, or for several hours, in a little water. Boil the milk and turn over the tapioca. Add, when it is blood warm, the sugar and eggs well beaten; bake about an hour, and after it has cooled a little, add the whites of the eggs to ¼ pound sugar for frosting. It answers well for a sauce, and looks quite ornamental.

Gelatine Pudding.
Fannie W., Aurora, Ill.

One ounce gelatine; 1 pint cold milk; set on range, and let come slowly to a boil, stirring occasionally; separate the yolks and whites of 6 fresh eggs; beat the yolks well and stir slowly into hot milk; add ½ a pound of granulated sugar; when quite cold stir in a quart of whipped cream, flavored with vanilla and lemon extract mixed; have the whites of the eggs beaten very stiff, and stir in the last thing; pack on ice.

Macaroni Pudding.
Jennie D., Joliet, Ill.

A quarter of a pound of macaroni broken into pieces an inch long; 1 pint of water; 1 tablespoonful of butter; 1 large cup of milk; 2 tablespoonfuls of powdered sugar; grated peel of ½ a lemon; a little cinnamon and salt. Boil the macaroni slowly in the pint of water (in a dish set in a kettle of boiling water) until it is tender. Then add the other ingredients. Stir all together, taking care not to break the macaroni; simmer 10 minutes. Turn it out on a deep dish, and serve with sugar and cream.

Plain Boiled Pudding.
Mrs. J. Y. S., Belvidere.

One cup sour cream; ½ cup molasses; ½ cup melted butter; 2½ cups flour; 1 teaspoonful soda; a little salt. Mix molasses and butter together and beat until very light; stir in the cream and salt, and then the flour gradually, until it is a smooth batter; beat in the dissolved soda thoroughly, and boil in a buttered mold an hour and a ½. To be eaten hot with sweet liquid sauce.

Sweet Potato Pudding.
Mary N., Elgin, Ill.

To 2 coffee cupfuls mashed sweet potato (boiled) add 1 teacupful sugar, 1 teacupful butter, 4 eggs, 1 teacupful sweet cream, 1 teaspoonful cinnamon, 1 grated nutmeg, 1 teaspoonful lemon (extract), and a pinch of soda dissolved in a teaspoonful of water. Beat the eggs light, add sugar and butter rubbed to a cream; stir all together into the mashed potato while hot. Cover a deep plate with puff-paste, and pour in the mixture. Bake in a moderate oven; when done, cover the top with slices of fruit marmalade, and sprinkle thickly with granulated sugar.

Baked Indian Pudding.

For a 2-quart pudding use 2 teacups meal; moisten the meal with cold water; then pour over it 1 pint of boiling water; add 1 tablespoonful of butter; 2 teacups of sugar; 1 cup of raisins; 3 eggs well beaten before adding, and fill up with sweet milk; season with whatever spice is preferred; bake slowly ½ an hour or more.

Carrot Pudding.
Mrs. M., Coldwater, Mich.

One cup of chopped carrot; 1 cup of mashed potatoes; 1 cup of chopped suet; 1 cup of sirup; 2 eggs; 2 cups of flour; spice to suit the taste. The carrots and potatoes are to be boiled first, of course—if the day before it will answer just as well.

Plum Pudding.
G. M., Tiffin, Ohio.

Two pounds of stoned raisins; 2 pounds well washed Zante currants; 1 pound sliced citron; 2 pounds finely chopped beef suet; 1 pound flour; 1 pound bread crumbs; 1 pound sugar; 1 nutmeg; 1 teaspoonful each of powdered cloves, allspice and cinnamon; the grated peel of a lemon, and 1 tablespoonful of salt. Mix these ingredients thoroughly. Add 10 eggs and sufficient milk to moisten to about the stiffness of fruit cake. Tie in a well-floured pudding cloth, and boil at least 8 hours. Serve with rich sauce.

Spiced Pudding.
Mrs. C. C., Warren, Ill.

Take 1 small square loaf of baked bread, peel off the crust, cut in pieces, and pour upon it 1 pint of boiling water, and add 1 teaspoonful of salt. Take 1 pint of flour; add 1 heaping teaspoonful of baking powder; 2 coffee cups of raisins, seeded and chopped; mix all well with the flour, first powders and next raisins; then add soaked bread and 1 teaspoonful each of allspice, cinnamon, mace and cloves. Then add by degrees 1 coffee cup of sweet milk, and beat the mass well together. Scald pudding bag, and put in the pudding, which should be pretty stiff, and boil 3 hours. The whole secret lies in plunging puddings in boiling water, immediately after they are mixed, and never letting them cease boiling. Be sure and turn them over, and always leave room in the bag for swelling. I have a wire basket made for holding puddings while boiling, made with legs, to keep them from the bottom of the kettle, so as to prevent burning.

Cottage Pudding.
Hattie, Aurora, Ill.

One cup sugar; 2 cups flour; nearly 1 cup of cold water; 1 egg; piece of butter size of an egg; 2 teaspoons of baking powder; salt. Sauce: One cup sugar; ½ cup of butter; mix thoroughly; add 2 cups boiling water; tablespoonful of corn-starch beaten with the butter and sugar. After taking from the stove, add 1 well beaten egg, and ½ lemon sliced. Cheap and good. A hot oven is necessary for the pudding.

Batter Pudding.
Mrs. C. C., Warren, Ill.

Four eggs—whites and yolks; 2 even cups flour; 1 pint of sweet milk; and 2 tablespoonfuls of baking powder; and 1 teaspoonful of salt. Mix the baking powder and the salt with the flour; beat the eggs, and stir in the milk, gradually at first, until the whole is one smooth mass. Scald a pudding bag in boiling water, put in the mixture, and plunge the whole into a kettle of boiling water, and boil 2 hours. To be eaten with cream and sugar.

Plum Pudding.

One quart of flour; 1 coffee cup chopped raisins; 1 teacupful of currants; 1 teacupful chopped suet; ½ cup candied lemon finely shred; 1 cup brown sugar; 1 teaspoonful of salt, and 2 of baking powder, and 2 cups of sweet milk. Sift the flour; put in the baking powder and salt, mixing thoroughly. Next add the raisins, currants and candied lemon, and incorporate well with the flour, so they will not sink to the bottom, as they will always do unless mixed first with the flour. Then put in suet and sugar, and lastly the milk, and, after stirring well, put in a bag which has been dipped in boiling water, and boil 3 hours. Do not let the fire get low so the pudding will stop boiling, and replenish always from a boiling teakettle. When done, put on a large platter, remove the strings, and turn the bag wrong side out—that is, pull it gently back and it will come off smoothly, if the bag is well scalded. Omit the lemon if you do not care for it so rich. Sauce: One cup sugar, ½ cup butter, 1 tablespoonful of flour, and 1 egg; melt the butter in the sauce-pan and stir in the flour until the whole is smooth; then stir in the egg, and pour upon this 1 pint of boiling water. By adding 3 tablespoons of brandy, it becomes brandy sauce, or the juice and grated rind of a lemon, it is called lemon sauce.

COOKERY—PUDDINGS.

Hotel Pudding.
Hattie, Aurora, Ill.

Boil 1 quart of milk; add ¼ cup of butter; 1 cup of corn-meal, mixed with cold milk; ½ cup each of sugar and molasses; 1 teaspoon cinnamon; 1 of ginger; 2 eggs; salt; ½ cup of raisins. Sauce, if you like.

Bannock Pudding.

One cup corn-meal; 1 of flour, well mixed; 1 cup sour milk; 1 egg; 1 tablespoon of lard; small teaspoon of soda.

Batter Pudding.
D. M. W., Jacksonville.

One pint of sweet milk; 1 tea (or coffee) cup of flour, and 2 eggs, beaten separately, the whites stirred in the last thing. And here is a sauce suitable for the same: One teacup of sugar; ½ a cup of butter—these rubbed together; 1 egg, separated—the yolk beaten with the butter and sugar; 1 pint of boiling water, thickened with a teaspoonful of flour or corn-starch; add to these the beaten white of the egg, and let it come to the boil; flavor to taste.

Egg Pudding.
Fannie, Kalamazoo, Mich.

Four eggs well beaten; 4 tablespoons of flour; add to the eggs until a smooth mass; then add a pint of milk slowly; a pinch of salt. Beat all smooth together. Put in a well-buttered dish, a bake about 20 minutes. Eat with sauce made of butter and sugar beaten together to a cream, flavored with vanilla.

Mrs. E. G., Geneva, Ill.

First boil soft 1 pound of raisins; then put 2 quarts of new milk over the fire; when nearly boiling, add ½ pint of corn-meal, wet up in ½ pint of cold milk; stir it till it boils; then turn it in your pudding dish, which must be large enough to hold 4 quarts. Then add 1 quart of dark sirup, ½ pound of butter, 5 eggs well beaten, 1 tablespoonful cinnamon, 1 teaspoonful allspice, ½ of a nutmeg, and ½ of a teaspoonful ginger. Then add the raisins, stir it up well; bake it in a slow oven for 3 hours. Let it cool 1 hour before eating. A smaller quantity than this will not be good, as it would dry out too much in baking. It is just as good cold as when warm, and it will keep sweet several days.

Boiled Indian Pudding.
B. Read, Belvidere, Ill.

One and one-half cups sour milk; 2 eggs, well beaten; 1 small teaspoonful saleratus dissolved in the milk; then sift in dry corn-meal until of the consistency as if for griddle-cakes (perhaps a little thicker). Stir in a teacup of dried fruit—cherries are the best. Put in a bag and boil 1 hour. For sauce, sweetened cream flavored with nutmeg.

Graham Pudding.
Blanche, Chicago.

Take a pint of water and allow it to boil thoroughly—not simmer—then salt, and stir in very slowly Graham flour—which must be fresh and sweet—until quite thick; after doing so, remove to the back part of the stove, and let it boil slowly for 15 minutes or more; it must be stirred at intervals to prevent burning. Served nearly cold with sirup or sugar and cream.

Delicate Pudding.
Aunt Mary S., Chicago.

One cup granulated sugar; 1 cup sweet milk; 1 egg; butter size of an egg; 1 cup raisins; 2 teaspoonfuls baking-powder; flour to make consistency of cake; steam in greased basin 1 hour.

Indian Pudding.
Mrs. Louisa T., Chicago.

Into a quart of boiling milk stir Indian meal enough to make a thick batter, with a tablespoonful of butter. When cool add 4 eggs well beaten, a tablespoon of ginger, a teaspoon of salt, and ½ a cup of sirup. Mix well, and bake 3 hours in a brown earthen dish, buttered.

T. M., Kendallville.

Put a quart of milk on the stove to scald; beat up 3 eggs, 3 tablespoonfuls of sugar, 3 of corn-meal, and a little salt. If it needs wetting more, add a little cold milk. When the milk nearly boils, pour in the mixture, and stir till it boils. Then set it in the oven and bake about an hour. Eat with butter and a little more sugar.

N. E. E., DePere, Wis.

One pint corn meal; ½ pint flour; 1 pint sweet milk; ½ cup molasses; 1 teaspoon saleratus; 1 teaspoon salt; steam 3 hours; pour it into a 3-quart pail and put the cover on; then set it into a kettle of boiling water, and keep it boiling—though the ordinary way of steaming would do.

Lemon Pudding.

R. Dubuque, Iowa.

One small cup butter 2 full cups sugar; mix very smooth, adding the grated rind of 2 lemons; yolks of 6 eggs; juice of the lemons, 6 small Boston crackers dissolved in 1 pint milk; bake. Make meringue of the 6 whites beaten stiff and 6 tablespoons powdered sugar. Spread on pudding and brown in oven. This needs no sauce.

Mrs. Mac, Kansas.

Two lemons grated; 2 cups sugar; 1 cup of cream; 2 tablespoons butter; 5 eggs; 3 tablespoons arrow root. Line a deep dish with paste, and bake ½ an hour.

Anna R., Pittsfield, Ill.

One large lemon, or 3 small ones: ½ a pound of sugar; ¼ a pound of butter; 1 coffeecup of cream or milk, and ¼ pound of butter; 6 eggs; 3 tablespoonfuls of grated cracker, or bread crumbs; beat the butter and sugar to a cream, grate the rind of a lemon, add juice, and yolks of eggs, and crackers; then the beaten whites of eggs and lemon. Sauce for the above: Mix well 3 tablespoonfuls of butter; add 1½ cups white sugar; then 2 eggs well beaten, and 1 gill of milk; put in a small bucket in a kettle of hot water, and let it thicken. Flavor with vanilla or lemon.

Delmonico Pudding.

Gracie Mayhuc, Hyde Park, Ill.

One quart milk; 3 teaspoons corn-starch, mixed with a little cold milk; 5 eggs—separate them, put the yolks with the corn-starch; add 6 tablespoonfuls sugar; put this into the corn-starch with the milk when boiling. Boil 3 minutes, or till cooked. Beat the whites to a stiff froth, and add 3 tablespoonfuls powdered sugar. Bake sufficient to hold the icing.

Florentine Pudding.
Aunt Lucy, Chicago.

Put 1 quart of milk into your pan ; let it come to a boil ; mix smoothly three tablespoonfuls of corn-starch and a little cold milk ; add the yolks of three eggs beaten ; ¼ a teacup of sugar; flavor with vanilla, lemon, or anything your fancy suggests ; stir into the scalding milk ; continue stirring till the consistency of starch (ready for use) ; then put into the pan or dish you wish to serve in ; beat the whites of the eggs with a teacup of pulverized sugar ; spread over the top ; place in the oven a few minutes, till the frosting is a pretty brown. Can be eaten with cream, or, is good enough without. For a change, you can bake in cups.

Chocolate Pudding.
Mary D. S., Elgin.

One quart milk, 14 even tablespoonfuls of grated bread-crumbs, 12 tablespoonfuls grated chocolate, 6 eggs, 1 tablespoonful of vanilla ; sugar to make very sweet. Separate the yolks and whites of 4 eggs ; beat up the 4 yolks and 2 whole eggs together very light, with the sugar. Put the milk on the range, and when it comes to a perfect boil pour it over the bread and chocolate ; add the beaten eggs and sugar and vanilla ; be sure it is sweet enough ; pour into a buttered dish ; bake 1 hour in a moderate oven. When cold, and just before it is served, have the 4 whites beaten with a little powdered sugar, and flavor with vanilla, and use as a meringue.

Vermicelli Pudding.

Into a pint and a half of boiling milk drop 4 ounces of fresh vermicelli, and keep it simmering and stirred up gently 10 minutes, when it will have become very thick ; then mix with it 3½ ounces sugar, 2 ounces of butter, and a little salt. When the whole is well blended pour it out, beat it for a few minutes to cool it, then add by degrees 4 well-beaten eggs, the grated rind of a lemon, and just before it goes into the oven a glass of brandy; pour a little clarified butter over the top; bake it from ½ to ¾ of an hour.

Sponge Pudding.

One-fourth pound each of flour, butter and sugar, 1 quart of milk, 12 eggs; mix butter, flour and sugar together, add to the milk, and boil until it thickens; when cool add first the yolks of the eggs, then the whites, beaten to a stiff froth. Place the pudding dish in a pan partly filled with water in the oven, and bake nearly an hour. For the sauce, ¾ cupful butter, 2 cupfuls sugar, and 1 of wine; mix butter and sugar to a cream, add the wine, a spoonful at a time, and put the dish in a pan of hot water to dissolve. This makes a light, delicious pudding.

Boiled Tapioca Pudding.
Contributor, Chicago.

Soak till quite soft 1 cup of tapioca; then boil in milk enough to make it like jelly—perhaps 15 minutes will suffice of steady boiling, constantly stirring; salt when put to soak. Pour out in molds, and eat with cream, and sugar and currant jelly.

Baked Tapioca Pudding,
Contributor, Chicago.

Soak 8 tablespoonfuls of tapioca in a quart of warm water or milk till soft; then add 2 tablespoonfuls melted butter, 5 eggs well beaten, spice, sugar and wine to taste. Bake in buttered dish and without lining.

Centennial Prune Pudding.
P. P. C., Chicago.

Heat a little more than 1 pint of sweet milk; when boiling, stir in gradually the following: 1 large spoonful corn-starch (or 2 of flour, if more convenient), mixed smoothly with a small quantity of cold milk; add 3 or 4 well-beaten eggs; enough sugar to sweeten; 1 teaspoon butter, and a little grated nutmeg. Let this come to a boil. Then pour it into a well-buttered dish, adding 1 teacup seeded prunes just before placing in the oven; bake about 20 minutes. The prunes must be previously stewed until tender. Serve with or without sauce as is preferred.

Bread Pudding.
Mary, Chicago.

Pour boiling water on a pint of dry bread-crumbs; melt with it 1 tablespoonful of butter. When soft, mix in two beaten eggs, 1 pint or more of fruit, stewed or fresh; sweeten to taste. It is better without spices. Bake 20 minutes, and eat with or without cream.

Steamed Dumpling.
Susan, Princeton.

Pare and quarter ripe, tart apples; place them in a deep dish, adding a little water; make a crust as you would tea-biscuit, of sour cream or rich buttermilk, if you have it; if not, any of the nice baking-powder recipes will do; roll about an inch thick; place over the apples, and steam ½ an hour. Serve with sauce made of ⅓ butter to ⅔ sugar, stirred to a cream. This dumpling may be made of any kind of fruit, fresh or canned.

Delmonico's Pudding.
Mrs. Mac, Kansas.

Heat a quart of milk to nearly boiling; reserve a little to wet 3 tablespoons corn-starch; beat up the yolks of 5 eggs, with 6 tablespoons sugar; stir these into the corn-starch, after being dissolved in the milk; then add to the hot milk, and boil 3 minutes; then add 1 teaspoon milk. Turn this into a buttered dish, and bake 10 minutes. Beat up whites, add three tablespoons white sugar and ½ teaspoon vanilla. Spread on pudding and brown. Eat cold with cream sauce.

English Plum Pudding.
Lizzie B., Marietta.

Nine eggs beaten to a froth; add flour sufficient to make a thick batter free from lumps; add 1 pint new milk and beat well; add 2 pounds of raisins stoned, and 2 pounds currants washed and dried, 1 pound of citron sliced, ¼ pound bitter almonds divided, ¾ of a pound brown sugar, 1 nutmeg, 1 teaspoon of allspice, mace and cinnamon, ¾ of a pound beef suet, chopped fine; mix 3 days before cooking, and beat well again; add more milk, if required. If made into 2 puddings, boil 4 hours.

116 COOKERY—PUDDINGS.

Tapioca Pudding.
J. A. S., Menasha, Wis.

One cup of tapioca; 1 quart of milk; soak 3 hours on the back side of the stove; when soft, and if too thick, add more milk; then ½ cup of white sugar; the yolks of 2 eggs; small spoonful of butter; a little salt and nutmeg. Bake slowly for an hour. Beat the whites of the eggs as frosting, and serve with pudding when done; or to be eaten as sauce, which I think is nicer than putting it on top of the pudding.

Sago Pudding.
J. A. S., Menasha, Wis.

Soak 1 cup of sago in warm water until it is all swelled alike; add water as it thickens, keeping it warm on the back side of the stove; when all swelled, peel 6 sour apples, core them, put them in the sago; sprinkle some sugar on top; bake until the apples are soft—say ½ an hour. To be eaten with cream and sugar.

Poor Man's Pudding.
Mrs. M. R. C., Manteno, Ill.

One cup molasses, 1 of sour milk, ½ cup butter or beef drippings, 1 teaspoon soda, flour to make as stiff as can be easily stirred. Use raisins as taste or purse dictate. Put in a spouted cake-tin and steam 3 hours. Eat with sweetened cream, or any sauce preferred.

Malagan Pudding.
Mrs. J. M. T., Chicago.

One-third cup of rice; 1 cup sugar; 2 eggs; 1 pint of milk; ½ a lemon and salt. Soak the rice over night. Beat the yolks of the eggs with one tablespoon of the sugar, and grate in the lemon rind; add the rice and milk. Bake 1 hour. Take the whites of the eggs and beat to a stiff froth with the rest of the sugar, then add the lemon juice. Pour it over the pudding after it is baked, and brown it in the oven 2 or 3 minutes. To be eaten cold.

Apple Pudding.
Frank, Chicago.

Make a plain crust with a little shortening in it, and cut in squares. Cut good sour apples in quarters, and put 3 of them in each square, after taking out the seeds. Then pinch the dough together, and put each one in a clean white muslin bag, and boil until they are done. Put on the table quite hot as a dessert. For sauce, boil good molasses with just enough butter. Pour into the gravy-boat and use.

"Amber's" Apple Pudding.
Amber, Highwood, Ill.

Take of apples that outblush the cheek of Hebe—6. Slice them thin as the shimmer of ice that flashes upon the bosom of your water pail in chill November. Grate a quantity of bread crumbs, fine as the drift of Sahara sands. Spread unto yourself within an earthen pudding dish alternate layers of apples and crumbs, sweetened with sugar and savory with nutmeg, yea, even moistened with water. And when the gentle heat of a moderate oven hath held your pudding one hour, or until the apple is soft as the cheek of happy infancy, eat ye of it, garnished with sweetened cream!

SAUCES FOR PUDDINGS, ETC.

Lemon Sauce.
Janet R., Racine, Wis.

THE juice of a nice soft lemon, some water, sugar till sweet enough, and a little whole cinnamon. Let this come to a boil, and pour a little in a cup, the well-beaten yolks of 2 eggs, with the "eye" of the egg removed, and when you have the cup filled with the boiling sauce (be sure and stir with 1 hand while pouring a little at a time in the cup till full), pour back in the pot, set on the stove, and let it come to a boil again, stirring all the while; then remove immediately and put in your sauce-dish to get cold. Beat the whites of the eggs very stiff with powdered sugar and put right on top of the sauce. Do not pour the sauce over the pudding till just ready to eat it.

Orange Sauce.
Mary B., Toledo, Iowa.

Place on the fire in porcelain saucepan ¼ of a pound of white sugar, ½ a pint of water, juice of 1 large orange, and the rind, cut off exceedingly thin; boil 5 minutes, strain, and add 1 glass of white wine.

Mrs. W. A. S., Arlington, Ill.

One coffeecup of sugar, ½ cup of butter, and 1 egg. Mix the 3 to a cream, and pour boiling water—1½ pints—over them, mixing well, after flavoring, with lemon or vanilla.

Another: 1 cup of sugar, an even tablespoonful flour and the same of butter. Mix to a cream. Put boiling water to them, and mix thoroughly, and put on the stove to cook, letting it boil 15 minutes, stirring occasionally. Flavor with grated nutmeg after taking it off the stove, and put in a little molasses, if you like it a nice brown color.

M. S. B., Kenosha, Wis.

Two cups coffee-sugar; 1½ of water, put over to boil; a heaping tablespoonful of flour, rubbed to a paste with butter as large as an egg; thin with the sirup while it is boiling, till it pours easily; then turn into sauce; let it boil a little; flavor with nutmeg, or brandy, if your conscience allows.

A nice cold sauce: Squeeze the juice of two oranges; add ½ a cup of sugar (more or less to taste); add a pint of cream or rich milk. This is nice, with cottage pudding, blanc mange, corn-starch, or any requiring cold sauce.

Biddy McBruiser, El Paso, Ill.

Yolks 5 eggs; 1 cup sugar; ½ cup butter; beat all together till light, and add slowly 1 pint of boiling water.

PANCAKES, FRITTERS, ETC.

Oat-meal Cakes.
Mrs. R. J. G., Onslow, Ia.

ONE cup oat-meal, wet with 1 cup sweet milk; soak over night; in the morning add a little salt, 1 teaspoonful baking powder, 1 egg, and enough sweet milk and a little cream to make as other gems; bake in gem-pans in a quick oven.

Buckwheat Cakes.
C. M. W., Hudson, Mich.

It will soon be time for buckwheat cakes. For the very best, make them ½ Graham; set them with yeast over night, adding a little sugar and salt. Use milk or water.

Breakfast Cakes.
J. A. S., Menasha, Wis.

One egg beaten very light; 1 cup of Graham flour; 1 cup of wheat flour; a little salt; sweet milk enough to thin them like griddle cakes. To be baked in irons heated hot before putting them in. This will make just 12. Be particular and beat the eggs very light.

Corn-meal Cakes.
Belle M. D., Chicago.

Take 2 cups of corn-meal, 1 cup of flour, a little salt. Mix well together. Two eggs well beaten; 1 pint of thick sour milk, in a little of which stir 1 even teaspoonful of soda. Mix well together in a batter, and fry on a well-greased griddle. The ladies need not be afraid to let their children eat them.

Apple Fritters.
Mrs. B. S. B., Arcola.

Pare, core and parboil some juicy tart apples in a very little water; chop fine; beat 7 eggs very light; add to them slowly ¼ of a pound of sifted prepared flour; beat very light; put in apple enough to thicken the batter, and the grated yellow rind and juice of a lemon; have the very best lard at a perfectly boiling point; put in it a thick slice of raw apple; put a large spoonful of the batter in at a time, and as many spoonfuls as the pan will hold; they take but a few moments to do and need not be turned over; must be made at the moment you wish to use them and sent to the table at once, each panful sent in as quickly as baked; powdered sugar with cinnamon and nutmeg in it, is nice for them.

Crushed Wheat Fritters.
Pansy, St. Joseph, Mich.

Take cold crushed wheat; 1 large tablespoon of flour; 1 tablespoon sugar. Mix all together with 1 egg well beaten; drop with a large spoon into good hot lard, and fry a nice brown. The best way to cook crushed wheat is to put it in a double boiler with water, boiling hot, enough to cover it. When well soaked, which will be in about $\frac{1}{2}$ an hour, mix up with milk and let it simmer $\frac{3}{4}$ of an hour.

Corn Fritters.
Mrs. S. B. C., Elgin.

Three ears of green corn; 1 egg; a little salt and pepper; flour enough to keep from separating in the fat. Fry as you do the rice fritters. Shave the corn thin, and scrape out the pulp. I used to grate it, but this is not so tedious and does as well.

Buckwheat Short-cake.
Ruby, Washington Heights.

Three cups sour milk; 1 teaspoon saleratus dissolved in the milk, with a little salt; mix up a dough with buckwheat flour thicker than you would for batter cakes (say, quite stiff). Put into a buttered tin, and bake in hot oven 30 minutes.

Oat Meal Cakes.
Young Grandma, Marshall Co., Ill.

Oat-meal can be made into mush, porridge, or set with rising, like buckwheat cakes, and baked on the griddle, only they will require much longer time in baking than buckwheat. It can also be used in making stir-cake, by using about ⅓ wheat flour.

S. S. B., Chicago,

Put 2 or 3 handfuls of meal into a bowl, and moisten it with water merely sufficient to form it into a cake; knead it out round and round with the hands upon the board, strewing meal under and over it until it is as thin as desired, and put it on a hot griddle, bake it till it is slightly brown on the under side, then take it off and toast that side before the fire which was uppermost on the griddle.

Graham Griddle Cakes.
Cousin Sarah, Canton, Ill.

Use the white wheat Graham, if possible. Equal parts of Graham flour and corn-meal stirred into sour buttermilk, or other sour milk, with a little butter added, soda and salt, and 1 or more spoons of sugar. Try them, and if sticky, the milk is too sour; add 1 or 2 eggs, or a little water. This is not a precise recipe, but I think no one will have trouble with it, especially as it can be varied considerably and still be good. I sometimes use all Graham flour: try it both ways, and I think you'll like them.

CUSTARD, BLANC MANGE, ETC.

Apple Meringue.
E. L. M., Chicago.

PARE, slice, stew and sweeten 6 tart juicy apples. Mash very smooth or rub through a sieve. Season with nutmeg or lemon-peel. Line a generous-sized plate with an under crust, and bake first. Whip the whites of 3 eggs—with 3 tablespoonfuls of pulverized sugar—till it stands alone. Fill the crust with apple, then spread the eggs smoothly over the top. Return to the oven and brown nicely. If you put your eggs in a dish of cold water a while before breaking them, they will beat up nicer.

Italian Cream.
Elma, Milwaukee.

Put the juice of 1 lemon and the rind of 2 to 1 quart of thick cream. Sweeten with ½ pound sugar, and let it stand for ½ an hour. Add 1 ounce of isinglass dissolved in ½ pint of water till perfectly smooth and free from lumps. Strain the whole mixture through a fine sieve and then beat together for several minutes. Put into a mold, and, when cold and perfectly set, turn upon a dessert dish.

Chocolate Cream.
Elma, Milwaukee.

One small cup of grated chocolate, 1 pound of sugar, 1 quart of milk, 1 box of Cox's gelatine soaked in ½ pint of water 1 hour. Boil all together 4 minutes; then add 1 pint of rich cream and boil 1 minute. Flavor with vanilla and pour into molds. This makes nearly 2 quarts of cream.

Snow Cream.
M., La Crosse, Wis.

Sweeten a pint of cream very sweet; flavor with vanilla or lemon as you prefer; let it stand where it will get very cold; when nearly ready for dessert beat new-fallen snow into the cream till stiff enough to stand alone; serve immediately.

Apple Snow.
Dorothea, Bloomington, Ill.

Prepare 8 medium-sized apples as for sauce; after it is cold, break the white of 1 egg in a dish; turn your apple-sauce over it, and whip with a fork 30 minutes. Care should be taken that each blemish be carefully cut away in preparing the apples, as the whiteness of the snow depends mainly on this.

Apple Puffetts.
Kenn Tucky, Macomb, Ill.

Two eggs; 1 pint of milk; sufficient flour to thicken, as waffle batter; 1½ teaspoons of baking-powder; fill teacup alternately with a layer of batter and then of apples chopped fine, steam 1 hour; serve hot, with flavored cream and sugar. You can substitute any fresh fruit or jams you like.

Charlotte Russe.
Dryad, Chicago.

One pint of cream; ⅓ of a box of gelatine; 2 tablespoons of sugar. Flavor to taste. Put the sugar in the cream before whipping it, then whip it until it is quite stiff and light. Pour cold water over the gelatine, and let it stand until all is dissolved. Then add the cream, and pour into a mold lined with slices of sponge cake. Stand in a cool place for a few hours. This recipe I use to line my mold with: 4 eggs; 2 cups of sugar; 3 cups of flour; 3 teaspoons of baking-powder; 1 cup of sweet milk. Beat the sugar and eggs together for 15 minutes. Stir in the sifted flour with the baking-powder. Add the milk, and bake.

Velvet Blanc Mange.
Bella, Kankakee, Ill.

Two cups sweet cream, ½ ounce Cooper's gelatine, soaked in a very little cold water 1 hour; ¼ a cup white powdered sugar, 1 teaspoonful extract of bitter almonds, 1 glass of white wine. Heat the cream to boiling, stir in the gelatine and sugar, and as soon as they are dissolved take from the fire, beat 10 minutes until very light, flavor and add the wine by degrees, mixing it well. Put into molds wet with clear water.

Irish Moss.
Mary, Peoria.

Soak a scant handful of Irish moss in strong soda-water until it swells; then squeeze the moss until it is free from water, and put it in a tin bucket which contains 6 pints of sweet milk. Set the bucket in a large iron pot which holds several pints of hot water; stir seldom, and let it remain until it will jell slightly by dropping on a cold plate. Strain through a sieve, sweeten and flavor to taste. Rinse a mold or a crock with tepid water; pour in the mixture, and set it away to cool. In a few hours it will be palatable. Eat with cream and sugar—some add jelly.

Velvet Cream.
Mrs. E. H., Chicago.

Take a package of gelatine and soak it in a cup of cold water till nearly dissolved; then place on the stove till heated through and thoroughly smooth (having added sufficient sugar to sweeten a quart of cream). Strain through a fine sieve, and add the cream when nearly cold, stirring until well mixed. Flavor of course—almond is very delicate—turn into a mold, and it will harden in a short time in cold weather. Some people use a cup of white wine instead of water, but it will be more apt to curdle.

Floating Island.
Lou, Tuscola, Ill,

Beat the yolks of 3 eggs until very light; sweeten and flavor to taste; stir into a quart of boiling milk; cook till it thickens; when cool, pour into a low glass dish; whip the whites of the eggs to a stiff froth; sweeten, and pour over a dish of boiling water to cook. Take a tablespoon and drop the whites on top of the cream, far enough apart so that the "little white islands" will not touch each other. By dropping little specks of bright jelly on each island will be produced a pleasing effect. Also by filling wine glasses and arranging around the stand adds to the appearance of the table.

Russia Cream.
Mrs. H., Odell, Ill.

Four eggs; 1 cup sugar; 1 quart of milk; ½ box of Cox's gelatine, dissolved in ½ pint of warm water. Beat the yolks of the eggs and sugar together, and cook with the milk (like custard). Take this off the stove; and add the (well beaten) whites of the eggs, stirring rapidly for a few moments. Now add the gelatine, and then a teaspoonful of lemon. Pour it into a pretty shaped dish to harden, and turn it out on a platter, and cut off in blocks (as ice cream). Make this cream the day before you want to use it.

Chocolate Blanc Mange.
Mrs. H., Odell, Ill.

One-half box gelatine, well soaked. Let 1 pint of milk come to the boiling point; 1 cup grated chocolate (not the sweetened); 12 tablespoons sugar. Add the gelatine just before turning into the molds. To be eaten when cold, with sugar and cream.

Apple Custard.
Aunt Sally, Springfield, O.

One pint sweet milk; 1 pint of smooth apple sauce well sweetened; 3 eggs; flavor with lemon and bake without top crust.

Apple Butter.
Aunt Sally, Springfield, O.

Take tart cooking apples, such as will make good sauce. To 3 pecks, after they are peeled and quartered, allow 9 pounds of brown sugar and 2 gallons, or perhaps a little more, of water. Put the sugar and water in your kettle, and let it boil; then add the apples. After they begin to cook stir constantly till the butter is done. Try it by putting a little in a saucer, and if no water appears around it the marmalade is ready for the cinnamon and nutmeg " to your taste."

Preserved Apples.
E. L. M., Chicago.

Pare and core 12 large apples; cut each into eights; make a sirup of 1 pound of sugar and $\frac{1}{2}$ a pint of water, and boil; put in as much apple as can be cooked without breaking; remove them carefully when tender; after all are done, add to the liquid 1 cup of sugar and boil 10 minutes slowly; flavor with lemon, and pour over the apples, or grate nutmeg on them instead.

Orange Dessert.
Algebra, Chicago.

Pare 5 or 6 oranges; cut into thin slices; pour over them a coffee cup of sugar. Boil 1 pint of milk; add while boiling the yolks of 3 eggs, 1 tablespoon of cornstarch (made smooth with a little cold milk); stir all the time; as soon as thickened, pour over the fruit. Beat the whites of the eggs to a froth; add 2 tablespoons of powdered sugar; pour over the custard, and brown in the oven. Serve cold.

Pennsylvania Apple Sass.
Maud, Urbana, Ill.

Take to 3 gallons of cider, 5 pounds of white sugar; 1$\frac{1}{2}$ bushels of apples. First boil and skim your cider. Let it boil $\frac{1}{2}$ an hour. Stew your apples in a portion of the cider. When your sauce is thick and glossy, add the cider and sugar. Season with cloves, etc.

Lemon Butter.
Lizzie S. E., Decatur, Ill.

For tarts: One pound pulverized sugar; whites of 6 eggs; and yolks of 2; 3 lemons, including grated rind and juice; cook 20 minutes over a slow fire, stirring all the while.

Ice Cream.
Palmer House, Chicago.

One quart rich milk; 3 eggs—whites and yolks beaten separately and very light; 4 cups sugar; 3 pints rich sweet cream; 4 teaspoons vanilla. Heat the milk to the boiling point; add the yolks and sugar, stirring well. Now add the hot milk, a little at a time, beating the whole time. Now set the dish inside another containing boiling water, and boil until thick as boiled custard, when pour into another dish to cool, after which beat in the cream, and flavor. It is now ready for freezing. Always use rock salt for freezing, as common will not do.

FRUITS, JELLIES, ETC.

Lemon Jelly.
Belle, Chicago.

DISSOLVE ½ box of gelatine in 1 cup cold water; grate 2 lemons; take off the thick skin and grate the pulp; put 3 teacups of water into a porcelain kettle; add 3 even cups of sugar; let it boil a few minutes, and then add the pulp and grated rind of the lemons, also the dissolved gelatine. Put into a mold and set in a cool place.

Wine Jelly.
Rella, Kankakee, Ill.

Two pounds white sugar; 1 pint sherry wine; 1 pint

cold water; 1 package of Cox's gelatine; juice of 2 lemons and grated rind of 1; 1 quart of boiling water; 1 good pinch of cinnamon. Soak the gelatine in the cold water 1 hour; add to this the sugar, lemons and cinnamon; pour over all a quart of boiling water, and stir until the gelatine is thoroughly dissolved. Put in the wine; strain through a double flannel bag without squeezing; wet your molds with cold water, and set the jelly away in them to cool.

Cider jelly is made the same way by substituting a pint of pure sweet cider for the wine. If you wish them colored, use the colored sugar, or a very little prepared cochineal.

Quince Jelly.
Mrs. E. H., Chicago.

Cover the fruit with water and boil until the goodness is all out (it will require $\frac{1}{2}$ or $\frac{3}{4}$ of an hour). Then strain through flannel or crash, without much squeezing. Strain twice if not clear; add equal quantities of juice and sugar and boil steadily about twenty minutes. It is better to leave the glasses several days before sealing, even if not quite hard, as your jelly will be much more delicate than if boiled too long.

Housekeeper, Chicago.

Wash the fruit; save all the nice parings and seeds; cook for an hour or more in more water than will cover them; then run them through the colander and let them sit until next day, or until the fruit substance has settled; now throw off the clear juice through a thin muslin bag, and sit on the fire; when boiling well add 1 pint of sugar to each pint of juice, and boil until it rolls off the spoon; fill the jelly-cups, and let them sit by the stove or any warm place a couple of days without covers, so as to evaporate any water if the jelly is not stiff enough.

Any jelly is better to be taken from the fire before quite done, as it will finish by sitting on the heater or near a warm stove, and if it boils 1 minute too long it will never be anything but a sticky, good-for-nothing kind of sirup.

Apple or any fruit jelly can be made by boiling the fruit (not skins and seeds) and treated in the same way.

128 COOKERY—FRUITS, JELLIES, ETC.

We have 40 glasses of different kinds, all clear as water, and *so* delicious!

Cranberry Jelly.
Amethyst, Chicago.

Two ounces isinglass; 1 pound double refined sugar; 3 pints well strained cranberry juice. Make a strong jelly of the isinglass; then add the sugar and cranberry juice; boil up; strain it into shape.

Crab Apple Jelly.
Little Sally, Jefferson, Wis.

Wash the apples, halve them, and cut out the blossom. Then put them into a porcelain-lined kettle and turn boiling water on them, but not enough to cover them (as some say), and cook them until very soft, stirring them occasionally to prevent burning. (Here let me say, that you need not be at all careful for fear of mixing the pulp with the sirup, as it makes no difference' whatever.) Next remove them from the fire and let them cool out some, and then put them into a bag made double from a piece of an old table cloth coarse and soft, and then put them into a large milk-pan and squeeze them. After squeezing out a little, empty them into the kettle, and so on doing, that they might not soak into the bag again. Now comes an important little item which I found out at the time, and did not know before. In consequence of having the bag double, I found that I could squeeze them very hard without any of the pulp getting through. You can easily tell when this part of the work is done. Then I put the juice into the kettle and boil it, removing the scum as it rises, until perfectly clear, and continue to boil it a few minutes longer. I then measure it, and there is 1½ quarts, and add just the same amount of sugar (granulated), and boil it a little over ½ an hour. You must "try" it before that time—put a little into a tin dish and set it into cold water. Make just a little allowance, for, after standing a day or two, it will be a little thicker than when you try it. If you find that your jelly is not thick enough the next day after it is made, you can turn it all back into the kettle and boil it over. Five minutes will make a great difference.

Wine Jelly.
Mrs. E. H., Chicago.

Wine jelly requires no eggs for clarifying if made from Cox's gelatine. Take 1 25-cent packet, juice of 3 lemons, rind of 1, and 1 pint of cold water; let stand 1 hour; then add 2 pints boiling water, 1¼ pounds white sugar, and a pint of sherry wine; turn into molds to cool, after straining. If you like cinnamon flavor, add a few drops of that extract. If you wish to make any other kind of jelly, omit the sherry and add orange juice, or anything you like. An elegant-looking jelly for company can be made in two colors by dividing when all ready for molding and coloring ½ with a few drops of cochineal (better procure it prepared at the druggist's). A third stripe can be made by dissolving a little gelatine in milk, but put no wine in, or it will curdle.

Each color must harden before adding the next, or they will run. The result is delightful, but it is rather slow work. The top ornament of blanc mange is much handsomer if colored with cochineal.

Stewed Cranberries.
Mrs. W. S. G., Baraboo, Wis.

One pound cranberries washed and picked over one by one, so as not to put in any soft or decayed ones; 1 pound granulated sugar; ¼ pint water. Place the water and sugar on the range to boil, stirring constantly; when boiling hot, throw in the berries—they will soon heat through and begin to burst; stir continually till well cooked; it will take about 10 minutes after all begins to boil; throw in a mold, previously dipped in cold water and not dried, and set till the following day. The above recipe makes the cranberries neither too acid nor too sweet—will invariably turn out like jelly—but is far nicer to eat with turkey, game, or poultry, as you have the full berry. I often prepare 10 pounds at a time, and it keeps perfectly, by pasting paper over the molds or bowls, 6 or 8 weeks. Always use porcelain kettles for cooking fruits in.

Spiced Citron.
Jane Eyre, Michigan City.

Prepare the fruit, cover with vinegar and let it stand

over night; in the morning pour off, and to every 7 pounds fruit allow 3¼ pounds of white sugar and a pint of vinegar; tie in a muslin bag a tablespoonful of each of the different spices; make a sirup of the sugar, put in the fruit and cook for ½ hour; when all the fruit is done add the vinegar and let the sirup boil thick; pour it over the fruit hot, and let it get cold before sealing up the jars.

Preserved Citron.
Mrs. L. M. G., Lawrence, Kansas.

Pare and remove the seeds, rejecting all but the solid part of the melon, cut in such pieces as you choose; weigh the pieces, and boil in water until you can easily cut them; remove the fruit, and add sugar to make the sirup, allowing 1 pound of sugar to each pound of fruit. When it boils, put in the fruit, and boil slowly 1 hour. When cold, add sliced lemon, allowing 1 lemon for 2 pounds of citron. 1 large teacup of water is the general rule for one pound of fruit.

Mrs. T. G. E., Chicago.

Pare and cut citron into ½ inch cubes, picking out all seeds. To 1 pound of citron 2 fresh lemons, and sugar equal to weight of lemons and melon. Boil the melon in clear water till very tender, skim out, and to same water add sugar; then boil till thick sirup. Cut the lemons in halves and boil in a very little water 20 minutes, then squeeze and strain the juice and water. Add the citron to the sirup and only let boil 15 minutes; also add the lemon-water 10 minutes before taking off. The citron toughens if cooked longer

PICKLES.

Mixed.
X. Y. Z., Hudson, Mich.

ONE colander of sliced green tomatoes, 1 quart sliced onions, 1 colander of cucumbers pared and sliced, 2 good handfuls of salt. Let all stand over night; then drain through sieve, and scald ½ cup celery seed, ½ ounce allspice, 1 teacup white mustard seed, 1 tablespoon black pepper, 1 pound brown sugar, 2 tablespoons mustard, 1 gallon vinegar, poured over hot.

Grape.
K., Galesburg, Ill.

Take ripe grapes; remove all imperfect and broken ones; divide the large bunches, as they will pack more closely; put in an earthen jar a layer of grapes and then one of grape leaves (the tannin in the leaves helps to preserve the firmness of the grapes). To 4 quarts of vinegar take 2 pints of white sugar, 1 oz. of cinnamon, ¼ oz. each of cassia and cloves. Let the vinegar, sugar and spices all boil together a few minutes, and, when quite cold, pour over the grapes. By pouring the vinegar over the grapes cold you avoid cracking the grapes, and they retain their natural form and color as long as they last.

Cucumbers.
C. M. W., Hudson, Mich.

To 1 gallon of soft water add 1 teacup of rock salt; heat it boiling hot; pour it over your cucumbers; let them remain in the brine 24 hours; turn off the brine; heat it again, and turn on the cucumbers the second time, and let them remain another 24 hours; and again the third time, when they will be ready for the cider vinegar, which must be poured over them cold; cover them with horse radish leaves to prevent mold rising on them; press them under the vinegar with a heavy plate, and in a few days they will be ready for use, and will keep green and bright all winter.

Sweet Cucumber.
C. M. W., Hudson. Mich.

Take small crock of pickled cucumbers and make a good rich sirup of New Orleans molasses, and cider vinegar, and whole cloves; heat together, and turn over them, and in 2 day you will have a most delicious, brittle, hard, sweet pickle.

Ripe Cucumber.
F. C., Chicago.

Remove the seeds and rinds; slice them an inch thick soak them in cold vinegar over night; drain off the vinegar and throw it away. Take 1 gallon of vinegar, 4 pounds of sugar a few sticks of cinnamon bark, and in this mixture boil the pieces of cucumbers, removing each piece as it becomes clear, without being broken—some pieces will be done before others, and place them in a jar, when all are removed to the jar, pour the boiling vinegar over them, and keep them under the surface.

Sweet Grape.
Mrs. J. P. H., Chicago.

To 8 pounds fruit use 4 pounds sugar and 1 quart of vinegar. Place the fruit in jars. Boil and skim the sirup, and pour over the grapes boiling hot. Repeat this process 3 or 4 days. Then seal up and set in a cool, dry place. Boil any kind of spices in the sirup that suits the taste.

Peaches.
Mrs. Sarah L., Chicago.

Take to 1 gallon of good cider vinegar 8 pounds of cut sugar. Let it dissolve in a large jar. Stick a clove into each peach. Put over the fire about a quart of the vinegar with the sugar dissolved, and drop in while cold 16 peaches, that will just fill a Mason's quart jar. Allow the peaches to boil slowly until a fork will stick easily through them. Oh, I forgot. You must put in a stick of cinnamon and a little allspice and cloves tied up in a rag. Not too much. It makes them black. Take out and carefully place in a jar, 1 by 1, fill with the liquid and screw on the top.

Picalilli.
Subscriber's Wife, Beloit.

One peck of green tomatoes, seeded; 2 large heads of cabbage; 3 green peppers; a small teacup of salt. Chop and mix well, and put in a colander to drain over night. In the morning cover it with good cider vinegar, and let it boil until soft. Then drain off that vinegar and put in tablespoonful of mustard, 1 of allspice, 1 of cloves ground, 2 pounds of sugar, and about ¼ a teacup of horse radish, and 3 onions if you like. Cover nicely with cider vinegar, and let it boil a few minutes. Put into a stone jar and lay on the top a thin white cloth. Put an old plate on to keep it under the vinegar.

Home-Made Vinegar.
Mrs. Sarah L., Chicago.

Take 6 gallons good cider; put this into a wine cask, and in the spring add 4 gallons of rain water, 1 gallon of molasses, and 4 pounds of sugar. Tear in small pieces a ½ sheet of brown wrapping paper to make " mother "; set the cask in the sun, and stick a glass bottle in the bung. In making currant jelly, I took the rinsings of the currants and poured that in, and a few peach-parings and stones, and cherries and blackberries, I poured in after soaking a day or so. This was the foundation of my vinegar, and that vinegar barrel has been kept working night and day ever since by adding more cider, more water, molasses and sugar.

Pickled Cabbage.
Mrs. Mac, Kansas.

Select a nice, firm head of cabbage; take off all the outside leaves and shave it exceedingly fine (not chop it, remember); place it in the jar you intend to keep it in, sprinkle salt and pepper on it to your taste; then cut a couple of red peppers very fine; add 2 tablespoons celery seed (or it is a great improvement, if you can get it, to chop up fine 2 heads of nice celery), 2 tablespoons white mustard seed; pour over cold vinegar enough to cover.

Chow Chow.
Mrs. Sarah L., Chicago.

Two quarts of small white onions; 2 quarts of gherkins; 2 quarts of string beans; 2 small cauliflowers; ¼ a dozen ripe red peppers; ½ pound mustard seed; ¼ pound whole pepper; 1 pound ground mustard, and, as there is nothing so adulterated as ground mustard, its better to get it at the druggist's; 20 or 30 bay leaves, and 2 quarts of good cider or wine vinegar. Peel the onions, halve the cucumbers, string the beans, and cut in pieces the cauliflower. Put all in a wooden tray, and sprinkle well with salt. In the morning wash and drain thoroughly, and put all into the cold vinegar, except the red peppers. Let boil 20 minutes slowly, frequently turning over. Have wax melted in a deepish dish, and, as you fill and cork up, dip into the wax. The peppers you can put in to show to the best advantage.

Chili Sauce.
Mrs. Louisa T., Chicago.

Take 2 quarts of ripe tomatoes, 4 large onions, and 4 red peppers. Chop them together; then add 4 cups of vinegar, 3 tablespoons of brown sugar. 2 tablespoons of salt, 2 teaspoons each of cloves, ground cinnamon, ginger, allspice, and nutmeg. Boil all together for 1 hour, and bottle for use after straining through a sieve or coarse netting. Is equal to famous Worcestershire.

Tomato Catsup.
Mrs. Sarah L., Chicago.

Boil 1 bushel of tomatoes until soft enough to rub through a sieve. Then add to the liquid a ½ gallon of vinegar, 1½ pints salt, 2 ounces of cloves, ¼ pound allspice, 3 ounces good cayenne pepper, 5 heads of garlic, skinned and separated, 1 pound of sugar. Boil slowly until reduced ½. It takes about 1 day. Set away for a week; boil over once, and, if too thick, thin with vinegar; bottle and seal.

Green Tomato Catsup.
Mrs. H. L. B., Chicago.

One peck tomatoes, 6 pods red peppers, or 1 teaspoonful pulverized, 4 tablespoonfuls salt, 4 tablespoonfuls black pepper, 1 tablespoonful mustard, 1 tablespoonful ground cloves, 1 tablespoonful allspice, 2 quarts white wine vinegar; cook tomatoes and peppers in vinegar until soft; then strain, adding all the spices, and boil slowly 5 hours; when cold, put in bottles and seal.

CONFECTIONERY.

Vinegar Candy.
Mrs. N. W. H., Chicago.

HREE cups sugar : 1 cup vinegar ; a piece of butter the size of an egg. Boil 20 minutes ; pour over plates to cool. Flavor, but do not stir.

Sugar Drops.
Helen Blazes, Chicago.

One pound of flour ; ¾ of a pound of sugar ; ½ pound of butter ; 4 eggs ; a gill of rose water ; bake on buttered paper in a quick oven. This makes 60 drops.

Cocoanut Drops.
Busy Bee, Ottumwa, Iowa.

Peel a cocoanut ; cut in thin slices ; cut these again crossways into threads about ½ an inch long ; add 1¼ pounds moist brown sugar ; 1 teacup of cold water, and the sliced nut ; put into basin and boil ½ an hour over slow fire, stirring frequently to keep from burning ; drop a spoonful at a time onto a coarse wet linen towel to cool.

Chocolate Drops.
Kitten, Warsaw, Ill.

I take 2 cups of sugar (white) to 1 cup of water ; after it has boiled 5 minutes, remove from the fire and place in plate or dish and stir briskly till cool enough to shape into balls, after which place out to get cold and hard. In the meantime grate ½ a cake of Baker's chocolate, which you place in a plate and put over the teakettle to melt, after which process you roll the balls in the chocolate, and then place out to harden ; and for butter scotch, take 1 cup of molasses, 1 of sugar, and a ½ cup of butter ; boil all together till to a candy.

Candying Orange.
Mrs. H., Ft. Wayne, Ind.

Peel and quarter them. Make a sirup of 1 pound of sugar to a pint of water, and let it boil until it comes to the candying point. Dip the oranges into this candied sirup and place them on a sieve to drain. Put this sieve over a long, flat dish, which will catch the dripping sirup, and let the oranges remain so in a warm place until the candied sirup upon them is dry and crystalized.

Molasses Candy.
Agnes H., Aurora, Ill.

Boil some molasses in a spider until it hardens on snow or cold water. When done, stir in soda until there is about twice as much of the candy as there was of the molasses, and a little lemon extract for flavoring. Care must be taken that the candy does not burn, or it will have a bitter taste. The soda makes it light and gives it a grain. Pour on buttered plates to cool.

[NOTE—The following recipe, if carefully followed, will prove perfectly satisfactory. It alone is worth $5 to any lover of candy]:

Chocolate Caramels.
Candy Maker, Chicago.

Take 4 ounces confectioners' chocolate; put it in a copper or iron kettle; put in a ½ dipper of water and stir over a slow fire until it dissolves; add more water if needed; then add 3 pounds of A sugar; ½ pint cream and ¼ teaspoon of cream-tartar; put them in with the chocolate and stir slow until it comes to a soft crack. To try it, dip a spoon in the kettle and then in the water. When done, pour in a small dripping pan; grease the pan before putting in. When cool, cut in squares to suit yourself.

YEAST, BAKING POWDER, ETC.

Baking Powder.
Mrs. J. B. J., Chicago.

SIX ounces of tartaric acid, 8 of the best baking soda, and 1 quart of flour; sift 5 or 6 times through a fine sieve so as to thoroughly mix the ingredients; always procure the materials from a good druggist; by so doing you have for 50 cents what would cost you $1 if you bought it from a grocer. Keep it well corked in a jar; use the same quantity as you would of any other powder.

Beer or Hop Yeast.
K., Galesburg, Ill.

Put 1 large handful of hops into your yeast-jar, and 1 large tablespoonful each of dark brown sugar, white flour and salt. Pour over these 1 quart of boiling water. Stir, and when luke-warm, put in ½ teacup of yeast. One-half teacup of this yeast, strained, will make 4 ordinary loaves of bread.

Hop Yeast.
Mrs. W. S. G., Chicago.

Grate 10 large potatoes raw; have ready 6 quarts of strong hop tea boiling; pour over the potatoes, stirring constantly, and let it boil a moment or two; add 1 coffee cup of salt and sugar each. When milk-warm rise with a pint of baker's or home-made yeast. Set in a warm place until done working. It will take a day or two to finish, but it stops after awhile.

Potato Yeast.

Take 12 common-sized potatoes, boil soft and mash hot; pour over 1 pint boiling water; add 1 pint cold water; strain through a colender; add 1 teacup sugar, 1 tablespoon salt. When cool add 1 teacup baker's yeast. Set in a warm place (not hot), allow it to rise light several times (say 4 or 5), and beat down. After which place in a glass jar, cover tightly, and set in a cool place. Half a teacupful of this is sufficient for 2 ordinary-sized loaves of bread. This yeast will not sour.

Potato Sponge.
Mrs. M. E. M., Evanston, Ill.

Six potatoes boiled; mash in a pint of flour; then pour on the boiling potato water to scald it. Stir, and let it stand until cool. Then add more water and flour to make the quantity you wish; add a cake of yeast soaked. Let it rise until bed-time. Give it a good stirring, and let it stand until morning, when it is very light and ready—3 cups for coffee-cake, 1 cup and a little water for a rye and Indian loaf, the rest for white bread and a pan of delicious biscuit. All but the coffee-cake are baked before dinner, and only 1 cake of yeast used. I use cans which have had tomatoes in them to bake the brown bread in. The loaf does not have as much crust, and cuts in pretty slices for the table.

MISCELLANEOUS.

Imitation Wax Candles.
Candle Maker, Chicago.

ONE pound of alum dissolved in warm water to each 5 pounds of tallow. Melt tallow; add the alum water; let water pass off in steam; run into molds. This will make the candles hard and look like wax.

To Sweeten Rancid Butter.
Butter Maker, Elgin.

Work the butter *thoroughly*, in sweet milk. If done as it should be, every particle of rancidity will be washed out.

Lemon and Orange Extract.

As the peel is removed from the fruit, cut it into

slices, put it into a large-necked bottle, and cover it with brandy or wine. As the liquor is used up fill the bottle, as the strength is diminished add more peel.

To Prevent Jars Breaking.
Mary Moore, Chicago.

When putting in the fruit I set the cold jar on a folded cloth wet with cold water; then fill with the boiling-hot fruit. I have never known a jar to break when thus treated.

Canning Corn.
Aunt Nancy, Joliet.

Make a salt brine strong enough to bear up an egg; put it in a ½ barrel or large crock; then put in the whole ears of corn without cooking, just as you husk them. When the barrel is full, put a clean white cloth next to the corn, then a piece of board fitted to the barrel inside, with a stone on it for a weight, just as for pickles. When you wish to cook the corn you must freshen it some, as you do salted pickles. Then either shave it off or boil it in the cob, a la summertime.

Canned Berries.

Heat slowly to boiling, in a large kettle, after adding 1 tablespoon sugar to each quart of fruit, and a little water to prevent burning on. Let all come to a good boil and can quickly. This is a good rule for all kinds of fruit.

Welsh Rarebit.
Hen Huzzy, Elgin.

We make a Welsh rarebit by melting good old cheese with a little vinegar, butter and milk, and pouring it over bread, toasted or untoasted, as we happen to fancy.

HOUSEHOLD HINTS.

To Fasten Colors.
Matilda, Chicago.

USE sugar of lead—about 2 tablespoonfuls to a pail of water—to wash all kinds of goods, from cotton to silk to prevent fading.

To Clean Painted Walls.
Jeanette, Danville, Ill.

Mix common whiting with water till about as thick as paste; apply with a flannel rag, and wash off with warm water and a cloth.

To Sweep Carpets.
Marian, Racine, Wis.

Wash, dry and chop potatoes, spread them on one side of the room, and sweep across the carpet.

To Remove Iron Rust.
Pickles, Ravenswood.

The juice of lemon and salt placed on the spot, and the fabric placed in the sun, will remove rust. Shining through glass its rays are stronger. I hang mine in a window.

To Clean Zinc.
Mrs. Kate G., Bryan, O.

Wet the zinc over with muriatic acid, sprinkle over it very fine sand or ashes, then scour, wash and dry. Or, rub with kerosene.

To Remove Fruit Stains.
Mrs. Kate G., Bryan, O.

Place your muslin over a tub, hold it firmly, and pour hot water through the spot stained and it will soon disappear. This must be done before putting the muslin in soapsuds.

To Polish Furniture.
Edna, Chicago.

Mix sufficient vinegar in linseed oil to cut it; with this, saturate raw cotton, over which place soft muslin; rub lightly over the article.

To Polish Metal.
Aunt Nancy, Joliet.

To polish copperware, tea-kettles, reservoirs, etc., use a teacup of vinegar and tablespoonful of salt; heat it hot and apply with a cloth, and rub till dry.

To Remove Mildew.
S. R., Chicago

Wet in rainwater; rub the spots with soap and chalk, lay in the sun and dew 2 or 3 days and nights. The spot should be *thoroughly* rubbed with the soap and chalk once or twice each day. I have tried this and found it effectual.

Shells.

Can be thoroughly cleaned by boiling in milk.

To Kill Mice.
Mrs. W. A. M., Niles, Mich.

Spread gas tar around the mice-holes, and you will have no further use for cats or traps.

I. N. P., Peoria.

Mix equal parts of fine corn-meal and plaster of Paris, and set it in dishes on the floor of the harness-room, and the mice will leave the harness and premises at once.

To Destroy Cockroaches.
D. W. M., Jacksonville, Ill.

I have been successful in driving away, if not exterminating, cockroaches by scattering powdered borax in their haunts.

To Remove Marble Stains.
Mrs. Will Killem, Chicago.

Take 2 parts of common soda, 1 part pumice stone, and 1 of finely-powdered chalk; sift through a fine sieve, and mix it with water to the consistency of paste; then rub it well over the marble, and the stains will be removed. Wash the marble afterwards with soap.

To Clean Silver.
Kate Somers, Chicago.

In cleaning silver, do not rub it away with scouring materials, but wash in hot water containing a good quantity of concentrated lye, or, if very black, boil for some time in soft water with a considerable amount of washing-soda added; then wash in a good suds, rinse in clear water, and rub with flannel cloth, or better, chamois-skin, and your silver will not often require cleaning, but will shine like new for a long time.

To Clean Gloves.
Polly Perkins, Chicago.

Buy 1 quart of gasoline at a lamp store, for 5 cents—a druggist would ask 20 cents for the same quantity. It will clean 4 pairs beautifully. Pour a small part, say an $\frac{1}{8}$, into a dry wash-bowl, put in 1 glove and wash immediately, just as though it were a soiled handkerchief, being careful to rub harder on the most soiled spots; rinse in clean gasoline; squeeze out (not wring), and in 10 minutes they will be dry. To remove the offensive odor, hang them up to air.

To Color Kid Gloves.
May Pearce, Chicago.

India ink, dissolved in water and applied evenly with a camel's hair brush, will give a jet black color. A $\frac{1}{4}$ of an ounce of extract of logwood in 2 ounces of brandy, will give a lilac; increase the proportion of logwood and a darker color is produced, even nearly black. Strong tea gives a handsome brown.

To Clean Oil Cloths.
Mrs. F. M. F., Chicago.

Wash with warm water; 150 deg. hot cracks the varnish. Soap is necessary in smoky districts, though it can not be used without dulling the colors somewhat. If a sponge is used, examine thoroughly for shells; they scratch the varnish. The dirt thus removed, rewash the whole with sweet milk and water; then wipe dry. The milk makes the surface smooth; dirt does not catch readily to it; the oil in the milk tends to restore the colors. Gentle friction with an old silk handkerchief will give a polish.

Renovating Fur.
Reader, Fon du Lac, Wis.

Take a large tin pan; put a pint of wheat flour in it; put the cloak in it; rub it thoroughly with the hands until the flour looks dark; then if the fur is not white enough, rub it again with more clean flour; then rub it with pulverized chalk—5 cents worth is enough. This gives it a pearly-white look. It is also good to clean knit nubias.

To Remove Ink Stains.
D. M. W., Jacksonville.

As soon as possible after the ink is spilled on the carpet, dip a clean sponge in milk, and sponge the ink spot, cleansing the sponge again in clean water before putting it again in the milk, so as to avoid smearing it; continue the operation until all the ink is out; then, of course, the milk can be washed out afterwards.

Perhaps every one does not know that the color taken out of black goods with acid may be restored by the application of liquid ammonia.

To Retain Colors.
H. Y. Z., Guttenburg, Iowa.

To keep the colors of muslins, calicoes, and ginghams bright for a long time, dissolve a piece of alum (the size of a shellbark), for every pint of starch, and add to it. This will keep the color bright a long time.

Cleansing Fluid.
Mother, Chicago.

Used to wash alpaca, camel's hair, and other woolen goods, and invaluable for removing marks on furniture, carpets, rugs, etc.: Four oz. ammonia; 4 oz. white castile soap; 2 oz. alcohol; 2 oz. glycerine; 2 oz. ether. Cut the soap fine; dissolve in 1 quart water over the fire; add 4 quarts water. When nearly cold, add the other ingredients. This will make nearly 8 quarts, and will cost about 75 cents to make it. It must be put in a bottle and stoppered tight. It will keep good any length of time. Take a pail of lukewarm water, and put in about a teacupful of the fluid, shake around well in this, and then rinse in plenty of clean water, and iron on wrong side while damp. For washing grease from coat-collars, etc., take a little of the fluid in a cup of water, apply with a clean rag, and wipe well with a second clean rag. It will make woolen look bright and fresh.

Excellent Paste.
Hugo, Hillsdale, Mich.

One ounce of gum tragacanth—select the white flakes; moisten a part of this (as the whole ounce will probably be more than you will want at once) with warm water; then reduce its consistency to suit your liking; if too thin, it will strike through unsized paper, and, when dry, will give the reading matter a dark and illegible appearance. Should your paste ever become dry from exposure, or, as it will in warm weather, become sour or moldy, moisten it as from time to time it may require with a little good vinegar.

Glue for Mounting Ferns, Etc.
Rella, Kankakee, Ill.

Five parts gum arabic; 3 parts white sugar; 2 parts starch; add very little water, and boil, stirring until thick and white.

To Make an Aeolian Harp.
Tom Cat, Springfield, Ill.

Of very thin pine make a box 5 inches deep, and 7 inches wide, and a length just equal to the width of the window in which it is to be placed. Across the top, near each end, give a strip of wood $\frac{1}{2}$ inch high and $\frac{1}{4}$ inch thick, for bridges. Into the ends of the box insert wooden pins to wind strings around—2 or 4 pins in each end. Make a sounding hole in the middle of

HOUSEHOLD HINTS.

the top, and string the box with blue violin strings. The ends of the box should be increased in thickness where the pins are inserted by a piece of pine glued upon the inside. It is better to have 4 strings, but a single string produces a very sweet melody of notes.

To Make Black Ink.
Chemist, Chicago.

Dissolve in an open vessel 42 ounces of coarsely-powdered nut-galls, 15 ounces of gum senegal, 18 ounces sulphate of iron (free from copper), 3 drachms aqua ammonia, 24 ounces of alcohol, and 18 quarts of rain water. Mix and let it stand until the fluid has assumed a deep black color, then bottle.

To Wash Flannel.
Harris & Cobb, Chicago.

After preparing suds of hot water and soap, wash the garment thoroughly with the hands (avoiding a wash-board or washing machine of any kind). When this is done, rinse in warm water containing a slight quantity of soap. Slightly wring the article thus cleaned and hang it up. Take it down while yet a little damp, and iron till perfectly soft and dry. Caution! Flannels or woolens of any description should never go into water too hot for the hands, or into cold water.

Washing Linen.
Louise N., Kenwood, Ill.

To wash fine linen so that it will retain its color, take as much hay as will color well the amount of water you wish to use; boil and rinse the goods in it, using a little soap. Be sure and use this preparation for both washing and rinsing.

To Clean Infants' Socks, Worsted Goods, Furs, Etc.
M., Cleveland, O.

Take a pan with a pint of white flour; rub the article in the flour well; shake the flour off out of doors; if there are soiled places still, put it in the flour again. It takes a good deal of rubbing with the flour. This will clean almost any knitted worsted article in white goods; also white lace ties, and it will clean white furs till they look like new.

Washing Black Goods, Linens, Etc.
Mrs. M. M. P., Chicago.

The best method of washing black (mourning) calicoes and dark brown cambrics, is to put a pint of wheat bran into 4 quarts of cold water; boil for ½ an hour; strain into a tub, and add sufficient warm water to wash 1 dress. Do not use soap. Rinse, and add blueing to your starch to prevent the white appearance starch leaves on dark colors. The bran softens the water. Wash brown linen in this way, adding a little hay to the bran-water while boiling. If there are grease spots on the linen use a little soap on them. Brown linen should not be dried in the sun.

Washing Clothes.
Old Housekeeper, Chicago.

Red-border napkins will bear boiling with other clothing, but scalding is all that is necessary, as, indeed, it is for all of the washing. For the last 12 years I have scalded my clothes instead of boiling them. Have the clothes washed as cleanly as possible, and add no soap for the scald. That in the clothes from the suds is all that is necessary. In an ordinary-sized wash-boiler of water add 1 tablespoonful of ammonia, and blueing as desired. Put the clothes in when cold, and let them just come to the boil and remove. Rinse and dry. The blue put in the scald gives a much clearer look than in the rinse, without looking blue.

To Iron Easily.
Aunt Nancy, Joliet.

Put a teaspoonful of kerosene into your cold starch, say to a pint, and your iron will not stick. The smell will soon pass off; rub your iron on soap or wax if it is rough.

To Clean Lace Curtains.
Aunt Nancy, Joliet.

To clean lace curtains without washing them: Shake the lace gently to remove the loose dust; then spread a clean sheet on a table, and lay the curtains 1 above the other with a plentiful sprinkling of unsifted cornmeal or bran between them. Then roll them up snugly, and put away in a safe, dry place for a week or 10 days; then shake the bran out, and with a moderately hot iron press out the wrinkles, and your curtains are as nice as new.

To Color Brown, Etc.
Marsh Mallow, Michigan.

To color brown: For 4 pounds of cloth or yarn, use 1 pound of cutch and 4 of bichromate potash. Dissolve the cutch in sufficient water to cover the goods, and boil them for ½ an hour; then dissolve the potash and dip the goods into the potash solution until the desired shade is obtained.

Scarlet: For cheap bright red suitable for rag carpets, 1 pound of Nicaragua wood; boil 2 or 3 hours; then add ½ a pound of alum; this will color 3 pounds of old flannel, or 2 of new. Let it remain in the dye 24 hours.

Green for woolen: To 1 pound of yarn or cloth, 2¼ ounces of alum and 1 pound of fustic. Steep to get the strength, but not boil; soak the goods until it acquires a good yellow color; then throw out the chips and add Indigo compound slowly until you have the desired shade. Rinse in cold water.

Polish for Linen Cuffs, Etc.
Aunt Jerusha, Valparaiso, Ind.

White wax, 3 ounces; spermaceti, 3 drachms; borax, 6 ounces; gum tragacanth, 1¼ ounces. Melt together with gentle heat. When you have prepared a sufficient quantity of starch in the usual manner for a dozen pieces, put into it a piece of the polish the size of a large walnut—more or less, according to the amount of washing. This will make a beautiful polish, and also make the goods very stiff.

Washing Fluid.
Housewife, Oconomowoc, Wis.

Here is a washing fluid I have used 6 years, and would not be without it: Take 2 pounds salsoda; dissolve; take 1 pound unslacked lime; boil it awhile; then set aside to settle; drain off, and add water to the amount of 2 gallons; add your salsoda; set aside for use. The night before wash-day, put your clothes to soak in warm soap-suds. In the morning put over your boiler, and to the boiler ⅔ full of water add 1 cup of fluid; wring your clothes from the tub; boil 15 minutes; then rub through 1 suds, and rinse. It bleaches, but does not rot the clothes.

Soft Soap.

Mrs. J. A. Pirie, Milwaukee, Wis.

Try out 14 pounds of grease; to this add 10 pounds of potash, dissolved in just boiling water enough to cover the lumps. In 2 or 3 days pour over the mixture several pailfuls of boiling water. (Be careful to use *boiling water*, as that cooks it). Keep on adding the water as fast as the soap thickens until your barrel is full of nice, sweet, clean soap. It must be stirred *hard* every time the water is put into the barrel, until it is entirely mixed.

Hard Soap.

Soap Maker, Chicago.

Take 1¼ pounds of clean, melted grease and 1 gallon of ley strong enough to bear an egg. Mix them together in a barrel and stir until a good soft soap is the result. Then take 6 quarts of this soft soap, 1 pint of salt, and a ¼ of a pound of resin; melt and scald the ingredients together, and put it aside to cool. When hard cut it, throw away the ley that has settled to the bottom and melt the soap again to refine it. Pour it into a small tub and when hard cut into cakes.

Lice on Canaries.

Mary, Vincennes.

To exterminate lice from canary birds, use hollow canes for perches; shake out well mornings into a cup of water, and you will catch them all. Two parts canary, 1 part rape, and 1 part hemp seed is the best food. The canes used are pipe stems.

To Kill Plant Lice.

Etta, Chicago.

Cigar ashes will kill lice on rose bushes without injuring the plants. I have tried it in many instances with great success.

Destroying Red Spiders.
Mrs. W. C. A., Lewiston, Ill.

Wash the plants once or twice a week in good strong soap suds—wash thoroughly every leaf on the under side with a sponge. Set the pot in a tub of washing-suds moderately warm, and throw the suds over them then.

Plant Lice Exterminator.
Dabbler, Green Bay, Wis.

Steep some quassia in water, and then pour over the plant, first washing the leaves with it. It is certain death to the lodgers, whether lice or worms.

Raising Canary Birds.
Bird Defender, Hillsdale, Mich.

Place the cage so that no draft of air can strike the bird. Give nothing to healthy birds but rape and canary seed, water, cuttle-fish bone, and gravel-paper or sand on the floor of the cage. No hemp seed. A bath 3 times a week. The room should not be over-heated—never above 70 degrees. When shedding feathers keep warm, avoid all drafts of air. Give plenty of German rape seed; a little hard-boiled egg, mixed with crackers grated fine, is excellent. Feed at a certain hour in the morning. For birds that are sick, or have lost their song, procure bird tonic at a bird store. Very many are guilty of great cruelty in regard to perches. The perches in a cage should be each one of a different size, and the smallest as large as a pipe-stem. If perches are of the right sort, no trouble is ever had about the bird's toe-nails growing too long. Keep the perches clean. The 14th of February is the proper time to place the male and female in the same cage.

Everlasting Whitewash.

Some years ago the following whitewash was used on the east end of the White House, and is as good to-day as when first applied: Take $\frac{1}{2}$ bushel of nice unslaked lime; slake it with boiling water; cover it during the process to keep in the steam. Strain the liquid through a fine sieve or strainer, and add to it a peck of salt, previously well dissolved in warm water

3 pounds of ground rice, boiled to a thin paste; ¼ pound of powdered Spanish whiting, and 1 pound of clean glue which has been previously dissolved by soaking it well, and then hang it over a slow fire in a small kettle within a larger one filled with water. Add 5 gallons of hot water to the mixture, stir it well, and let it stand for a few days covered from dust. *It should be put on hot*, and for this purpose it can be kept in a kettle on a portable furnace. It is said that about a pint of this mixture will cover a square yard upon the outside of a house if properly applied. Fine or coarse brushes may be used, according to the neatness of the job required. It answers as well as oil paint for wood, brick, or stone, and is cheaper. It retains its brilliancy for many years. There is nothing of the kind that will compare with it, either for inside or outside walls. Buildings or fences covered with it will take a much longer time to burn than if they were painted with oil paint. Coloring matter may be put in and made of any shade desired. Spanish brown will make a reddish pink, when stirred in, more or less deep, according to the quantity. A delicate tinge of this is very pretty for inside walls. Finely pulverized common clay, well mixed with Spanish brown, makes a reddish stone color; yellow ochre stirred in makes yellow wash, but chrome goes further, and makes a color generally esteemed prettier. It is difficult to make rules, because tastes differ. It would be best to try experiments on a shingle and let it dry. Green must not be mixed with lime; it destroys the color, and the color has an effect on the whitewash which makes it crack and peel.

THE TOILET.

Tooth Powder.
Dentist, Chicago.

MIX equal portions of powdered chalk and charcoal, adding a small quantity of curd soap. This simple recipe not only cleanses the teeth, but is a preserva-tive against decay.

To Whiten and Soften the Hands.
Mary B., Terre Haute.

One-half pound of mutton tallow, 1 ounce of camphor gum, and 1 ounce of glycerine. Melt, and when thoroughly mixed, set away to cool. Rub the hands with this every night.

To Remove Freckles.
Uncle Ben's Niece, Kentland, Ind.

A very simple and harmless remedy for freckles is equal parts of pure glycerine and rosewater, applied every night and allowed to dry.

To Remove Hair.
Paul H. B., Madison.

Quicklime, 30 parts; orpiment, 4 parts, powdered gum arabic, 60 parts. Mix and keep in a tightly-corked bottle. When used mix with water, so as to form a paste. Apply, and let it remain for 5 or 10 minutes, when the superfluous hair can be removed with the back of a knife. The following is a rather safe depilatory, and in some respects equal to the former: Take a strong solution of sulphuret of barium, made into a paste with powdered starch. Use as in the preceding one. This latter recipe, however, must be used immediately after being mixed, as it loses its efficiency if kept long.

To Prevent Hair Turning Gray.
Paul H. B., Madison.

Take the hulls of butternuts, say about 4 ounces, and infuse in a quart of water for an hour. Then add ½ an ounce of copperas. Apply with a soft brush every second or third day. This preparation is harmless, and is far better than those dyes made of nitrate of silver.

To Cure Dandruff.
Paul H. B., Madison, Wis.

Dandruff generally comes from an overheated or feverish state of the scalp. The cure is simple. Brush it well every day; apply a mixture of bay rum and brandy; avoid much oiling, and wash quite often with an egg and soft, tepid water.

French Curlique.
Paul H. B., Madison, Wis.

Oil of sweet almonds, 1 ounce; spermacetti, 1 drachm; tincture of mastich, 3 drachms. Dissolve the spermacetti (white wax is as good) in the oil with a slow heat, and then add the tincture. Apply a small quantity when the hair is to be dressed. This preparation is entirely innocent.

Hints About the Hair.
Paul H. B., Madison, Wis.

The yolk of an egg will thoroughly cleanse the scalp and make the hair soft and glossy—that is, if soft water be used. Beware of soap, for the potash it contains is very objectionable.

At least 20 minutes each day should be used by those who suffer from thin and weak hair in brushing it with a stiff brush. Before beginning this, apply every day a small quantity of the following: Tincture of cantharides, ½ ounce; bay rum and cologne, of each 2 ounces; and 1 drachm of oil of rosemary. Do this for a month, and the hair will be found to have improved wonderfully. Ladies who have, and do not like, red or blonde hair, will find their hair has grown much darker. The weak hairs, by this process, grow stronger, and the coarse ones fall out, causing the hair to become healthy and curly. The following method will cause bright red hair to become dark brown, or chestnut-hued: Take oils of nutmeg and rosemary, 1 drachm each; castor oil, 1 ounce; tincture of cantharides, 2 drachms; strong brandy, 7 ounces. Mix. Wet the hair with a small portion of this once a day, and brush the hair well with a stiff brush for ½ an hour by the clock, and ask your lover at the end of 5 or 6 weeks if he does not want a fresh lock of your *new hair*. This everyday brushing of the hair is worth more than all the " curling fluids " and other like humbugs ever invented.

Care of the Hair.

When the hair grows scantily, naturally, the following lotion may be used 3 or 4 times a week, in the morning: Eau-de-Colonge, 2 ounces; tincture of cantharides, 2 ounces; oil of rosemary and oil of lavender, of each 10 drops. When the hair becomes thin from illness, or other causes, use the following recipe: Mix equal parts of olive oil and spirits of rosemary; add a few drops of oil of nutmeg, and anoint the head very sparingly before going to bed. When actual baldness is commencing, use the following pomade: Macerate a drachm of powdered cantharides in an ounce of spirits of wine. Shake it well during a fortnight and then filter. Take 10 parts of this tincture and rub it with 90 parts of cold lard. Add a little essence of bergamot, or any other scent. Rub this pomade well into the head night and morning. In 99 cases out of a 100 this application, if continued, will restore the hair. When the hair, after being naturally luxuriant, begins to grow thin, use the following recipe: Take of extract of yellow Peruvian bark, 15 grains; extract of rhatany root, 8 grains; extract of burdock root, and oil of nutmegs (mixed), of each 2 drachms; camphor dissolved with spirits of wine, 15 grains; beef marrow, 2 ounces; best olive oil, 1 ounce; citron juice, ¼ a drachm; aromatic essential oil, as much as sufficient to render it fragrant; mix; shake into an ointment. Two drachms of bergamot, and a few drops of otto of roses would suffice. This is to be used every morning.

To Make the Hair Grow.
Mrs. Will Killem, Chicago.

Salt and water will not only prevent the hair from falling out, but if applied every day will bring out a fine growth of soft new hair. Should not be made so strong as to leave white particles upon the hair when dry.

For Itching Scalp.
Mrs. Eve, Kalamazoo.

One teaspoonful of ammonia, 1 of tincture of arnica, and 1 tablespoonful of soft water. Use this amount for 1 thorough sponging and rubbing of your head, and brush till dry. If badly diseased, use twice a week. Prepare just what you want for one application each time.

For Diseased Scalp.
Aunt Nelly Bly, St. Joe, Mich.

Buy 25 cents' worth of pine-tar; take 2 tablespoonfuls and put in an old quart bowl, pour on this 1 pint of boiling soft water; let stand till cool; remove the scum, and pour off in a bottle and cork, and use thoroughly every morning to wet the hair and scalp. It will surely cure you. My husband has used this for 2 years, and now his hair is thick and soft, and has hardly a gray hair; besides, the scalp is clean and healthy. Keep your tar-bowl always filled with water, and pour off when needed; put in a little more tar every 2 months or so.

All About Preserving and Improving the Complexion.
Paul H. B., Madison, Wis.

All the so-called "Balms," "Blooms of Youth," etc., are composed of white lead, glycerine and rose-water. For a time such preparations do seem to whiten the skin, but in a short time it loses its elasticity from paralysis of the small nerves, and becomes of a dirty, yellowish color. This invariably is the result of the application of all the cosmetics containing lead.

Still, there are a number of harmless articles which can be used as cosmetics, such as milk of roses, lac sulphur, glycerine, bay rum, bitter almonds, oatmeal water, and, if a mineral *must* be used, let it be sub-nitrate of bismuth. A few years ago the following sold in Paris for $5 a bottle: Pure glycerine and water, of each an ounce; vinegar of cantharides, 40 drops. The cantharides slowly destroys the rough, outer skin, and leaves the under soft and velvety. Madame Vestris used to sleep with her face done up in a mixture of the whites of eggs, sweet almond oil, and alum. This keeps the skin soft, but firm, and retards wrinkles. Gowland's Lotion is an excellent preservative of the complexion, and is made of 1 ounce of emulsion of bitter almonds, and 1½ grains of bi-chloride of mercury. If this be applied once a day, on retiring, and the face washed in tepid water, on rising, with the following soap, no lady need have a poor complexion long. The soap is made as follows: A pound of bleached castile soap, 4 ounces of fresh, sweet almond oil, 6 ounces of oatmeal. Place on the stove in a kettle, and keep stirring until all the ingredients are well incorporated. Then let it cool, and it is ready for use. The highborn ladies of England are noted for the beauty and whiteness of their hands. They use the soap above given. Glycerine is capable of making the skin soft, but it will not whiten it any. The following is the recipe for "Sultana," a deservedly-popular cosmetic with the titled ladies of London: Take 2 ounces of bitter almonds, blanche, and beat into a paste with 1 ounce of rosewater; then add honey, fine oatmeal, and glycerine, 1 ounce each, and when well mixed, 2 drachms of tincture of benzoin. Apply before a fire a short time before retiring. For rendering the complexion soft, smooth, and brilliant, this preparation has no superior. The following is good, and has the merit of being more easily prepared than the "Sultana." It is the French *pate au miel*, or honey paste: Take glycerine, honey, and rosewater, 2 ounces; subnitrate of bismuth, 4 drachms, and tincture of benzoin, 2 drachms. This is to be applied at night, and can also be used in the morning instead of soap.

And now for that torment of so many fair females—

freckles. In many females of a sanguine temperament, freckles, even if removed for a time, will be sure to return, and, therefore, may be said to be incurable. But in 9 out of every 10 cases the following will effect a cure: In the morning on rising, take a teaspoonful of lac-sulphur in a few teaspoonfuls of milk. Then, for external use, apply the following: Corrosive sublimate, 4 grains; alcohol, 1 ounce. Mix. Remember, ladies, that this latter mixture ought not to come in contact with the lips. After a few days' using, the skin will begin to very slowly peel off, and the freckles disappear. Twice daily is sufficient to apply it. A French dermatologist recommends the following for the same purpose: Take muriatic acid, ½ ounce; alcohol, 1 ounce; rain water, 7 ounces. Mix and apply well with a sponge 3 times daily. When in England, a Gypsy woman informed me that she used horseradish, boiled in milk, for removing freckles. She cured a number of young girls, but whether or not she told me the real secret of the means employed, I am unable to say, having never given the preparation a trial.

Cold Cream.
Helen Blazes, Chicago.

Take an ounce of rosewater; 2 ounces of oil of sweet almonds; ½ an ounce of spermacetti; 1 drachm of white wax; melt together in a bowl placed in a pan of water, *boiling*. Then remove from the fire, and stir until cold.

For those who prefer "something easier": One ounce glycerine; 1 ounce rosewater; 10 drops carbolic acid. This is a healing lotion, excellent for sore gums as well as "chaps"—and *other* excoriations.

Black-heads, Flesh-worms, Etc.
Pug, Mattoon, Ill.

They are permanently removed by washing with warm water, and severe friction with a towel, and then applying a little of the following preparation: Liquor of potassa, 1 ounce; cologne, 2 ounces; white brandy, 4 ounces. The warm water and friction are sometimes sufficient.

Care of the Hands.
Paul H. B., Madison, Wis.

What is called cream of roses is also an excellent preparation for the hands, either in winter or summer. It is made as follows, unless you prefer to purchase it at a $1 a bottle: Take compound tincture of benzoin, ½ an ounce; almond and Malaga oil, of each an ounce; ottar of roses, 5 drops; honey, 2 ounces; and enough rosewater to make the mixture measure 6 ounces. Apply as often as you like.

A mixture of lemon-juice and powdered borax is also another fine whitener of the skin, but should only be used in warm weather. This is admirably suited to those ladies whose general health is not good and who have, consequently, bluish hands, in which the blue veins show too strongly.

Ladies who do their own housework are apt, if they do not wear gloves, to have coarse hands. If they happen to dip them into water, they do not take time enough to dry them well before going on with their work. To wipe the hands perfectly dry after their being immersed in water, is imperatively necessary, if they wish their hands to look white. To keep the hands from chapping in cold weather, use a mixture of glycerine, 1 ounce; spermacetti, 2 drachms; olive oil, 2 ounces. Mix together with the aid of heat. Apply this every night, and, if time will admit of it, every morning. In winter, do not wash them in cold or hot water. It should be just blood warm, and no more or less. Do not go out of doors with them uncovered. In summer, use cold water, unless the hands perspire very much, as the hands of some people do. These latter should use tepid water. In warm weather, a good preparation for the hands is this: Take ½ an ounce of powdered alum, the whites of 2 eggs, and mix together. Then add enough bran to make into a thick paste. Apply this once a day, after washing, and after rubbing the hands together well for a few minutes, wipe off with a soft towel. This will give them a soft, brilliant hue, and check any undue amount of perspiration.

THE SICK ROOM, ETC.

Catarrh Remedy.
Medico, Chicago.

EQUAL parts of gum arabic, gum myrrh, and bloodroot, made into a powder, and used as a snuff, is an unfailing remedy for catarrh.

Chilblain Lotion.
Dr. Foot, Chicago.

Dissolve 1 ounce of muriate of ammonia in ½ a pint of cider vinegar, and apply frequently. One-half pint of alcohol may be added to this lotion with good effect.

Removing Warts.
Ella Hosmer, Danville.

Get at the drug store 5 or 10 cents' worth of oil of cinnamon; wet the warts thoroughly three times a day till they disappear.

Hot Water for Bruises.

Bruises and injuries do much better when treated with hot than cold water. The temperature should be about 103° Fah.

Bands for Children.
S., Chicago.

If the bowel complaint should become troublesome, keep a flannel band bound snugly around through all the hot weather. It supports the bowels, keeps them warm, and will often cure the trouble when medicine and diet have been of no avail.

THE SICK ROOM, ETC.

Care of Sick Children.
Mary Moore, Chicago.

I find that diet, bathing and quiet are the most effective remedies I can use. I took a child safely through measles, whooping-cough and teething with only common sense and general knowledge of the laws of health to guide me.

This time the children had a remittent fever—cold chills alternating with fever. When their feet were cold and heads hot, I applied hot water to the feet and cold water to the head. When the fever came on I sponged off the whole body with cool water, wiping lightly with a soft towel. I kept them on a light diet of such articles as would keep the bowels open—oatmeal, Graham crackers, etc. If this was not sufficient, I gave warm water injections. I kept them quiet as possible in mind and body, making them sleep all they could. And this treatment, with the blessing of God, brought them through all right.

Croup.
Isadora, Monroe, Mich.

As soon as my little ones begin to choke up and cough like croup, I bind a napkin wet with cold water, and a dry one over it, around the throat, and give a good dose of sirup of ipecac. The cloths must be changed every few minutes till the choking is over. If necessary, give the ipecac or hive sirup till the child begins to vomit.

Cough Medicine.
Anna R., Pittsfield, Ill.

One-half ounce essence of peppermint; ¼ ounce essence of cinnamon; ¼ ounce of laudanum; 2 ounces of paregoric—mixed with the same quantity of molasses. Dose: A teaspoonful to a tablespoon 3 or 4 times a day, or oftener if the cough is very bad.

Dyspepsia Remedy.
Sympathizer, Peoria.

On 2 tablespoonfuls of unslacked lime pour 1 quart of cold water; let stand a few minutes; bottle and cork, and when clear, it is ready for use; put 3 tablespoonfuls in a cup of milk, and drink any time, usually before meals, but between if the food sours or stomach pains.

Drinks for Invalids.
Annie M. Hale, Chicago.

Take crusts of genuine brown bread (rye and Indian). These should be slowly toasted before an open fire until thoroughly dried and of a rich, dark brown. Break them into small bits; put them into the coffee pot; pour on boiling water, and let the infusion steep from ½ an hour to an hour. Let the pot stand a few minutes after being removed from the fire. The coffee will be clear and of a fine color, and if served with rich milk or cream, can hardly fail to please an unspoiled palate. It is nutritious and innocent. A tablespoonful of ground Mocha or Java put in the coffee pot 10 minutes before it is taken from the fire will give it both flavor and aroma. The crusts of whatever bread may be used in a similar manner.

Corns, Bunions, and Ingrowing Nails.
A Friend, Normal, Ill.

Acetic acid is a safe and painless remedy for corns and bunions. A few applications night and morning will dispel all soreness. A continued application will remove them. Inverted toe-nails can be cured without causing any pain, by simply making a notch in the center of the end of the toe-nail in shape of the letter V. It causes the sides of the nail to come above and over the flesh. Continue this as fast as the nail grows out, and it will always keep its proper shape and position.

How to Get Fat.
Mrs. Sophia F., Chicago,

If you will try my recipe I think you will succeed in getting fat. I drink every day at 10 a. m. and at bedtime a glass of lager beer with eggs. It is prepared in the following manner: Take the yolk of 1 egg and 4 teaspoonfuls of white granulated sugar; beat well and fill the glass with beer. It is an agreeable drink, and will make any one what I am now getting to be—fat.

www.ingramcontent.com/pod-product-compliance
Lightning Source LLC
Chambersburg PA
CBHW030305170426
43202CB00009B/874